The Older I Get the Better I Was

An aging athlete looks back

By Mike Ransom

Copyright © 2021 by Michael Ransom
All rights reserved

*Dedicated to my family and all others
with whom I've become friends through sports*

Contents

Just Do It 1
Baseball 3
*My bloop single broke up a (would be)
major league pitcher's perfect game*
Ping Pong 23
Father, son, and lots of hollering
Volleyball 27
Too tired for amorous adventures
Slow-Pitch Softball 35
They called me "Wheels"
Football 41
Lamar Hunt and I watch his Kansas City Chiefs
Cross-Country Skiing 51
Fifty-five kilometers with 7,000 Scandinavians
Tennis 57
How I stopped running around my backhand
Racquetball 63
My best sport
Squash 79
I won't give it up until I'm old
Golf 83
Not one but two Masters Tournaments
Bicycling 99
A ride where I almost bought the farm
Hiking 117
A premonition haunts a hike
Running 123
Still running after all these years
Keep on Keeping On 133

Just Do It

The thought of writing this book has lingered in my mind for many years. My love of—and devotion to—a multitude of sports seemed to be a meaningful slice of my life I should record for posterity. My countless hours practicing, playing, and competing have reflected who I am and shaped who I've become. The COVID-19 pandemic that reared its ugly head in early 2020 and the sheltering that followed provided me time to write. I spent hours and hours going through boxes of scrapbook items, newspaper clippings, photographs, journal notes, and more and organized them into thirteen sports categories that would become the book's core chapters. I created a detailed life timeline, and I contacted friends with whom I had "sported" to help me fill in gaps and answer questions about events that took place long ago. The chapters stand on their own, so they can be read first to last or sampled at random.

One of the best things about writing is that in reflecting I've been able to relive some of the best moments of my sporting life. It's the summer of 1965. I'm batting lead-off and playing second base for my high school baseball team. We win the conference championship (first time in school history) and go on in the postseason tournament to beat a team 1–0 in extra innings; their pitcher eventually made it to the major leagues. I broke up his perfect game in the seventh inning with a bloop single and played probably the best game of my life. It's 1981 and I'm playing my heart out in the city racquetball singles championship against my doubles partner, seventeen years younger than me, someone I had taught to play the game. I'm running in my only marathon, jumping in at midstream to encourage my friend Ron Fess and run a few miles with him. Rather than encourage him, I develop a splitting side ache and feel I need to drop out, so it's Ron who has to encourage me. I'm jogging with Lamar Hunt, owner of the Kansas City Chiefs, around Arrowhead Stadium the morning before his team plays the Denver Broncos, a contest I'll be watching with him in his owner's box. It's Sunday at the 2019 Masters Golf Tournament. I'm there to see Tiger Woods make one of golf's most amazing comebacks. I'm standing with friend Frank Earnest on the South Rim of the Grand

Canyon looking across the twenty-four miles to the North Rim. The following morning we begin a two-day hike from North to South. I remember wondering (and worrying) if I could make it. The memories go on and on. It has been fun looking back.

I recall writing a memoir for a delightful man, Berdine Erickson, who was eighty-six at the time. When we finished, he thanked me for my help with his writing journey. "You made me feel young again," he said. Writing this book has done the same for me, and this has made the effort seem worthwhile. The book title I chose came from a quote by professional golfer Chi Chi Rodriguez. As we grow older, we sometimes exaggerate our past accomplishments and remember ourselves to be a little bigger, better, and stronger than we actually were. I've tried not to do that, though, in these remembrances, so any exaggeration is unintentional. I've learned that accomplishment is relative. In racquetball, for example, I was one of the best in the city, but I couldn't hold a candle to the best at the state and national levels.

I have written this book mainly for myself to help me remember the stories I've shared. I would be pleased if my family and friends with whom I've played all these sports might find it worthwhile to read, too. Maybe my granddaughters—Greta, Ellie, and Hattie—will someday find it of interest, to help them know some of what this old guy, their "Gpa," could do in his younger years.

Baseball

My bloop single broke up a (would be) major league pitcher's perfect game.

A photo from the 1966 Clear Lake High School yearbook. The caption reads, "Mike Ransom starts the '66 season with a hit, while Dave Pike waits his turn to bat."

I can't pinpoint where I was or at what age when I first held a baseball in my hand, oiled up a glove, or swung a bat. There aren't too many photographs of me playing baseball. One of my favorites is with cousins Bob and Rick Forzano taken on a diamond in their hometown of East Liverpool, Ohio. I'm maybe five. The catcher's mitt I'm sporting is much too big for me, but I've got a smile on my face that says I'm having fun. In my hometown Clear Lake, Iowa, I remember playing baseball games in Joe Jensen's backyard when seven or eight. Joe lived kitty-corner across the alley from our house. His older brother, Craig, played, probably Miriam Eastman (our neighbor across the alley), and Bill Farnan. Often, we would have pickup games at the Lincoln School playground with even more kids. I remember

I became hooked on baseball at a young age. Here I am with my cousins Rick and Bob Forzano in East Liverpool, Ohio.

swinging a black bat with white tape wrapped around the handle. I'm right handed, but I batted from the left side. Dad may have taught me that, seeing how I was pretty quick, and knowing that from the left side of the plate you have a step or two of advantage over right handers to get down the line to first base. I can see Dad pitching to me at Grandma and Grandpa's farm. Home plate was in front of the garage. If I swung and missed or didn't swing, the ball would bang off the closed door. On nearly every summer Sunday, I played baseball games with my cousins on that diamond. (Cousins included Curt, Barry, Doug, and Cathy Johnson and Mark and John Ransom.) Home was in front of the garage, first base at the corner of the barn, second base toward the milk house, and third base near the fence that surrounded the farmhouse yard. I loved playing shortstop and would field ground balls and fire them to first, knowing that an errant throw could shatter

THE OLDER I GET THE BETTER I WAS

a barn window and draw my grandpa's ire. Talk about pressure. (Grandpa was gruff, but seldom angry.)

Like many other young boys who loved playing baseball, I worshipped major league ball players and collected (and traded) baseball cards. Topps was the major card company when I was growing up. I initially liked the Chicago Cubs, maybe because of that cute bear on their player cards, but somewhere in the 1950s I became a Brooklyn Dodgers fan. My cousin Curt was a Milwaukee Braves fan. When it came to card collecting, he had an unfair advantage. A candy and sports card vendor, Mr. Anderson, lived on the corner just a few doors down from his house, so Curt could get complete sets of Topps baseball cards from him each year. This guaranteed that he would have a card for every player, even the All Stars. I, however, had to buy the nickel packs with the stiff-as-a-board sticks of bubble gum to try to cobble together a complete set by the end of the season. I never did. So, when Curt and I got together to compare our collections and trade cards, his was always far more complete than mine. In the mid-to-late 1950s, the Braves and Dodgers were two of the best teams in baseball's National League. I'm sure Curt needled me when the Braves won, and I probably needled him when the Dodgers came out on top.

After the Dodgers moved to Los Angeles in 1959, I continued to root for them. I have small spiral-bound notebooks in which I recorded the scores for every game the Dodgers played in 1961, 1963, 1964, and 1965. Wins were noted in red pencil. Our radio couldn't pick up the Dodgers' home games (too weak a signal plus they started late, around 9:00 Central time). When they were on the road, I listened to their games in Pittsburgh (KDKA), Chicago (WGN), and St. Louis (KMOX). What a treat it was on summer evenings to hear their action live.

I played in the town youth leagues at Lions Field starting when I was in fifth or sixth grade. The main field we used had a backstop behind home plate and bases; it was the field where Dad played fastpitch softball. A backstop on wheels was available to define an additional playing field. I recall most often playing shortstop and sometimes catching. Our team traveled to other towns. Dad told of arriving late to one of my games in Thornton. As he drove up to the field, I was rounding third heading home, having hit one well past the outfielders.

My dad had been an outstanding baseball player in his high school. He liked to tell the story of playing on a town baseball team one summer. He had forgotten his baseball socks, so his legs were bare below his knees. His first time at bat, the opposing team's catcher took a look at him and said, "Nice legs, Esther." (Esther Williams was a world-class swimmer and an attractive Hollywood actress.) Dad didn't say anything, but he proceeded to smash a couple of doubles and a triple in his first three at bats. On his fourth time to the plate, the catcher said, "Ok, nice hitting, Ted!" (Ted Williams was probably hitting close to .400 that summer for the Boston Red Sox.)

My dad was an excellent baseball player. He passed his love for the game on to me.

I owe much to Dad for helping develop my baseball hitting, throwing, and fielding skills. He provided as much encouragement as instruction, and I never felt any pressure from him to do well. He spent hundreds if not thousands of hours with me hitting fly balls and ground balls on the diamonds at Lions Field, pitching batting practice, and standing in our backyard behind a homemade (by him) home plate catching my pitches. Dad hit fly and ground balls to me until his hands bled. I had a pretty strong arm, and I loved rifling throws from the outfield back to him at home plate. Now that my arm is shot, I think longingly of the frozen ropes I threw, like one might pine for a long-lost girlfriend. (Sports I was good at; dating is another story.) After taking flies in the outfield, I'd come in to second base, and Dad would hit grounder after grounder, which I'd fire back to him at home. When we hung it up, I'd be dripping with sweat. Sometimes, we'd drive to State Park or City Beach and jump in the lake to cool off on our way home.

Playing catch with Ben while vacationing in Lutsen, Minnesota

I love the *Field of Dreams* movie that came out in 1989. I can't watch the final scene without a lump forming in my throat. In the movie, Ray Kinsella (Kevin Costner) builds a baseball field in the middle of an Iowa cornfield. He isn't sure why, but he does it anyway. He finds out at the end of the movie that the reason for doing so is to reunite with his father, John, who had died years before. They had had a falling out, something that Dad and I never had. But at the end, when Ray steps onto the baseball field, realizes his dad is there, and asks, "Hey, Dad, you wanna have a catch?" I can't help but tear up. I think of the balls Dad hit me at Lions Field that helped me make the high school team as second baseman. I think of the times we played catch over the years until one year his arm just couldn't throw any more. I think of my son, Ben, who even today will ask, "Dad, how about a catch?" As I look back, something strikes me that I hadn't realized before. Take the "g" out of "glove" and what's left? It's "love." Playing catch and hitting grounders was much more than just playing catch and hitting grounders. It was more than baseball. It was Dad's way of showing his love for me.

High School Baseball: The Clear Lake Lions

While I was in high school, Dad worked his regular job as a maintenance man at Northern Natural Gas, and to make additional money, he helped Grandpa on the farm and painted houses. (I worked with him on the latter two.) He always found the time and energy for our baseball workouts. Now that I'm older, I realize how tired he must have been prior to some of those sessions. But I never, ever felt he wasn't enthused about the time we spent together on a baseball diamond.

Mom and Dad (Barbara and Jim) were my biggest fans. Mom was a good athlete in her day and had played softball. She told the story of pitching in one game when a batted ball hit her in the face and broke her nose. Dad would tell of sitting in the stands with her during one of my games when a fan of the opposing team began making some snide remarks about my height, or lack of it. When Mom had heard enough, Dad said she reached over and pulled the guy's hat down over his eyes. Mom (and Dad) would never think of bragging about me, but they sure stood up for me.

Our high school played summer baseball. I tried out for varsity my freshman year and made the team, which Gus Brandt (our math teacher) coached. I don't have our year-end win–loss record, but I batted twelve times, had three hits, and lettered. (I would letter all four years.) I was so excited; you would have thought I had made the big leagues. Seniors on the team included Harold Bostrom and Larry Mix. Don Anderson and I were the only freshmen to make the team. (Don was also an outstanding basketball player. He would make the Iowa Basketball All State Team his senior year.) Letter jackets were big back then. I remember buying mine at one of the two Clear Lake sporting goods stores (Satter's or Clark's, which were across from each other on Main Street) and how proud I was wearing it with my letter "C" sewn on.

The next summer, in 1964, we won twelve and lost seven. I played second base, had nineteen hits (for a .288 average), scored twenty runs, and had a team-leading sixty-six at bats. Seniors included Tom Buck,

Dave Kofoed, Bob Mosiman, Lauren Tapps, and Gary Mestad. Other sophomores on the team with me were Don Anderson, Jim MacDonald, Mark Schoneman, and Chuck Vega. Butch Skovgaard of Sheffield pitched a no-hitter against us; we lost eleven to nothing.

The summer of 1965, between my junior and senior years, was most memorable. We not only won the conference championship, but the All-Star Game was played in Minneapolis (Met Stadium), Sandy Koufax (my baseball hero) pitched a perfect game, and the Los Angeles Dodgers and Minnesota Twins (my two favorite teams) squared off in the World Series. Over the past fifty-five years, I've often reflected on that summer. If I could choose one "youthful" time to relive, that would be it.

Clear Lake Lions 1965 Baseball Conference Champs. Don Anderson and I are the first two on the left in the front row.

We finished at the top of the eight-team North Central Conference with a record of six wins and one loss, the first time Clear Lake had won the title. I hit a lead-off homer against Webster City (a line drive down the left-field line that kept rolling as I zipped around the bases). We won the game 9–5 and upped our conference record to four wins and no losses. I fielded the final out for the win over Clarion (9–5) that gave us the conference championship. Our overall record was seventeen wins and five losses. I batted lead-off, played second base, and hit .315. I led the team in games (22), at bats (73), runs (27), hits (23), stolen bases (8), and bases on balls (17). We had a talented bunch of seniors. Senior starters included Tom Berge, Les Cookman, Tom Keenan, Tom Anderson, Denny Warren, and Dick Dillavou. Don Anderson, Jim McDonald, and I were the junior starters. Berge and Cookman were best friends who kept the team loose. On road trips, they would lead us in singing the Herman's Hermits' song "I'm Henry the Eighth" (second verse, same as the first!) and do other goofball things to make us laugh. Tom was an excellent baseball player, quarterbacked the football team, and played guard for the basketball team. His father, Earl, was the Clear Lake schools' superintendent. Sadly, in 1970 Tom was killed in a car accident near Algona on his way to Clear Lake from Mankato, Minnesota, where he was working on his master's degree. He was only twenty-two, with a bright future in store. Some said that Earl was never the same after Tom's death. Les Cookman named his son Tom to honor the memory of his best friend.

Following our regular season, we played in the sectional tournament; the winner would move on to the state tournament. At the time, there were no classes in which schools of similar sizes were grouped. We won our first game 1–0 in ten innings over Rockwell-Swaledale in one of the most exciting sporting events I've ever participated in. We played at Mason City's Roosevelt Field, which, to me, was like playing in a big league stadium. We were deemed the visiting team. The newspaper account indicates that I "touched" their pitcher Don Eddy for a single in the top of the seventh inning to break up his perfect game. He had set us down in order up to that point. I can still see that "touch," a blooper that barely avoided the shortstop's outstretched arm. Eddy struck out twelve of us before he left the mound after nine innings (per high school rules limiting pitchers to that

Box score of our tournament win over Rockwell-Swaledale

number). Our lanky Don Anderson matched Eddy pitch for pitch, giving up only two hits and no runs through the first eight innings.

Don Eddy, a flame-throwing lefty who would make it to the major leagues, pitched against us in the 1965 sectional baseball tournament. I broke up his perfect game with a bloop single in the seventh inning, and we beat his team 1–0.

Denny Warren relieved Don to start the bottom of the ninth and held the other team scoreless. We scored the only run of the game in the top of the tenth off reliever Harold Bergman, who walked two batters, Denny and another, to start the inning. With one out, Denny stole third and came home on an errant throw by their catcher. In the bottom of the tenth, Denny got two outs and then Don Anderson came back in (he had another inning he could pitch) to get the last out. I considered myself an average-fielding second baseman—I had the second-most errors on the team for the season—but I was in a zone that night, getting eleven assists, if memory serves me. After we recorded the last out, Coach Brandt came out of the dugout onto the field and shook my hand, congratulating me on such a fine game. Coach Brandt was a good guy, but he was gruff and looked like a Marine drill sergeant. He was not generous with compliments, and this made his postgame gesture even more meaningful to me. Don Eddy went on to pitch for the Chicago White Sox in 1970–1971, so I have been able to claim that in my baseball-playing days I got a base hit off of a pitcher who would make it to the major leagues!

I doubt if Eddy ever thinks of that game. If he does, I'm sure it's not as fondly as I do. We beat Nora Springs 11–1 in the following game. I was three for four with two RBIs and two runs. Our luck ran out, though, in the next game, and we lost to Mason City 11–0. Mason City was a town of 35,000 people to Clear Lake's 5,000. If there had been team classes, I think our team could possibly have won the state title that year.

The summer after my senior year, 1966, we finished with three wins and four losses in the conference and nine wins and ten losses overall. My stats weren't as good as the year before. I played in thirteen games and batted .224 in fifty-eight at bats. The personal highlight of the season was my grand slam home run to help us beat conference foe Eagle Grove 9–6. We were behind 6–4 in the fifth when I hit it.

My four years on the baseball team, all coached by Mr. Brandt, taught me much about teamwork, practice, performing under pressure, winning, and the true joy of the game. I loved every minute of every game. The following spring, I tried out for the Iowa State baseball team but didn't make the cut. Had I not tried out, I would have always wondered if I had been good enough to make the team. Though I didn't expect to be picked, I gave it my best shot.

Visits to Cooperstown

An IBM business trip to White Plains, New York, in October 1988 offered me (and Dad) the chance to visit the Baseball Hall of Fame in Cooperstown. When I learned of the trip, I immediately thought of combining business with pleasure, and when I asked Dad if he'd like to come along, he agreed in a split second. We flew to White Plains and rented a car. 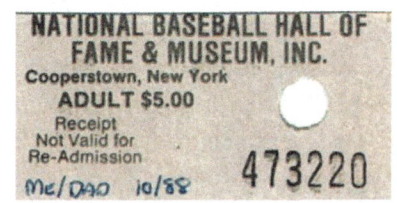 On our four-hour drive to Cooperstown, the fall colors were at their peak. We made an afternoon of it at the Hall of Fame, and then drove back to White Plains where, in our Rye Town Hilton hotel room, we watched the Dodgers beat the Mets 6–0 in the National League

12

playoffs. Only a week later, the Dodgers would beat Oakland in the first game of the World Series, one of most thrilling series games of all time. The Dodgers went up early 2–0 on a Mickey Hatcher home run, and then Jose Conseco put the A's ahead in the top of the second with a grand slam. The Dodgers scored a single run in the sixth inning. In the bottom of the ninth, with a runner on and two outs, pinch hitter Kirk Gibson, who was so hobbled by an injury he could barely walk, came to the plate to face Dennis Eckersley, the best reliever in baseball, and with two strikes on him hit a walk-off two-run homer. The Dodgers won 5–4 and went on to win the series. For a Dodger fan, things could not get better.

In October 2010, Jeanine and I vacationed in Cooperstown. We toured the Hall of Fame and the Fenimore Art Museum. There's such a charm to the village of seventeen hundred that Jeanine and I fell in love with it and hope to get back someday for another visit.

Coaching Baseball
For ten summers, starting in 1989 when Ben was eight, I had the privilege of coaching the baseball teams he played on, moving up with him and his team each year. During much of this time, I was a member of the Rochester Youth Baseball Association (RYBA) Board of Directors and, for several years, in charge of coordinating the umpiring for all of the youth baseball games. I served as the board's secretary, too. I have so many memories of those years; to do them justice would require a separate book. I made this note after Ben's first game:

> 5/31 1989: My first game coaching Ben and his T-ball team. What a neat feeling watching him play. He hit two home runs, a triple, and a double. He played great in the field and threw out all three batters on ground balls back to him at the pitcher's mound in the top of the last inning. He ran like crazy around the bases. He was the best player on either team. What wonderful memories!

RYBA leagues were separated into majors and minors. Most kids dreamt of playing on the majors. Each spring, coaches held tryouts for their teams to select the fourteen or so (from the dozens who tried out) for the team. The toughest part of my coaching each year was informing those who hadn't made the team.

My coaching career got off to a rough start. Our fourth grade team's home field was Soldiers Field, we were sponsored by Gillespie Sporting Goods, and our record for the season was four wins and twenty-one losses. There was no place to go from there but up.

The end-of-season party for our fourth grade baseball team. From their smiles, you would never know we finished with four wins and twenty-one losses. I learned much about patience during that season. Ben is kneeling on the far left.

Though our roster did not contain the same players each year, we steadily improved such that our seventh grade team won the city championship. Here's my assistant coach Dave Langevin's account of the final game:

The game for all the marbles and we came away with the prize. We beat Virgil's (coached by Dave Ruud) for the third time, avenged our only loss, and finished the season at 19–1. It wasn't easy.

The game was tied at 3–3 after 5 innings; we won by scoring single runs in the 6th and 7th. Pitching by both teams was excellent. Their pitchers held us to 8 hits, walked only 3, and struck out 5. Our pitchers (Travis Dee and Collin Nash) allowed just 4 hits, walked 2, hit 1, and struck out 6.

We got a big break in the first inning and jumped to a 2–0 lead. After Matt (Buzzell) walked and Ben (Ransom) lined into a double play, Collin hit a line drive that their 2nd baseman dropped. Joe (Ties) followed with a home run over the center-field fence. It was Joe's 4th home run of the playoffs and 10th of the year. Virgil's got one run back in the bottom of the 1st on a lead-off triple and, after 2 out, an infield hit to deep short.

We loaded the bases in the 2nd on singles by Max (Bahr) and Lucas (Koerner) and an error on Travis's grounder, but failed to score. Virgil's also threatened in the 2nd, but Joe, in center field, threw the batter out at 1st on a base hit to shut them down.

Virgil's tied the game at 2–2 in the bottom of the 3rd, but Joe came to the rescue again by throwing another batter out at 1st on a base hit to center. Both teams had a runner 3rd with only one out in the 4th, but good pitching prevented any scoring.

We took a 3–2 lead in the top of the 5th. With 2 outs and no one on base, Joe got an intentional walk. Tyler (Melton) came through with a triple down the right-field line to put us ahead, but only for a few minutes. Virgil's tied it again on 2 singles, a wild pitch, and an error.

We scored what proved to be the winning run in the top of the 6th. Lucas walked, stole second, and scored on Nathan Matusiewicz's double down the left-field line. Collin pitched real tough in the bottom of the 6th, getting 2 strikeouts and a grounder to 3rd.

We added an insurance run in the top of the 7th. With 2 outs and no one on base, Tyler doubled to the fence in right center. Max followed with a single to left, Tyler scoring just before Max was thrown out at 2nd trying to stretch his hit into a double. Collin was tough again in the bottom of the 7th, getting 3 infield outs. Buzzy made 2 fine plays at short, and Max got an unassisted out at 1st. It was a very exciting game, well played by both teams. We were just a little bit better. League champions in the regular season and now playoff champions—truly a memorable year!

What a satisfying feeling as a coach to see your players reach the top through hard work, hustle, and good play. We finished with sixteen wins and one loss during the regular season and won the City Championship with wins over Arby (21-6), Police (18-4), and Virgils (5-3). The team had an overall .411 batting average and a total of thirty-three home runs. There were more than two thousand players involved in the RYBA summer program. What an honor to have our team come out on top of the 7th Grade Majors. I tried to instill in my players that sportsmanship was equally as important as winning. In addition to RYBA games, I coached traveling teams that played several weekend tournaments each summer. The RYBA program ended after eighth grade. I moved on to coach Ben's VFW team the summers of his freshman and sophomore years. I owe a tremendous thanks to my co-

coaches over the years: Craig Allen, Mike Baudoin, Terry Buzzell, Neath Folger, Hal Henderson, Joe Koerner, Dave Langevin, Jim Sanyo, and Bob Suk.

Our 7th Grade Majors team finished the regular season with sixteen wins and one loss and then won three games to claim the City Championship. These guys could play baseball! Ben is on the far right in the first row.

One of the reasons I enjoy baseball so much is that you never know when you'll see something in a game that you've never seen before. In one summer tournament in Apple Valley, our traveling team played a powerhouse team from a Twin Cities suburb. Their team could hit the cover off the ball. Ben was in seventh or eighth grade and played left field. A big bruiser lined a ball to him; Ben fielded it on one hop and glanced up at the lumbering runner, and I could see the thought entering his mind that he could throw him out at first. "Don't do it!" I thought. I had taught our right fielders to always be on the watch for throwing a runner out at first, which several did. As Dave Langevin noted, in our RYBA championship game, Joe Ties threw out two runners at first base from *center field*. Ben, therefore,

Ben was an excellent outfielder, hitter, and base runner, but he could throw a mean curveball, too.

had seen such aggressiveness pay off. Just as I was thinking "no way," Ben fired a rope from *left field* to our first baseman that got the guy out at first. The runner was as amazed as the rest of us. In my lifetime of watching baseball at all levels, I have never seen such a play made.

Ben played on the Mayo High School varsity team and the American Legion Team his junior and senior years. He was a much better hitter (right handed) than I, a speedy base runner, a good pitcher, and an excellent outfielder. Never in my baseball (or slow-pitch softball) career did I hit an over-the-fence home run. (Our high school home field didn't have a fence over which to hit a ball.) Until his sophomore year, Ben hadn't either. One spring afternoon, Jeanine and I watched his junior varsity game in Northfield. In his first or second at bat, he hammered a pitch over the left-field fence. He circled the bases somewhat surprised at his feat, while Jeanine and I clapped loudly from the stands. Wow, his first home run! In Ben's next at bat, on the very first pitch, I'll be darned if he didn't hammer another home run over the fence. Back to backs! He circled the bases, again somewhat sheepishly, and jogged back to the bench to receive high fives and back slaps from his teammates. Those would be the only two fence-clearing home runs he would hit in his baseball career—two more than I hit. Word traveled fast about Ben's two swings. The Mayo varsity was playing at the time on a nearby field. After the game, Mike Restovich (the star of the team, who played in the majors for six years, including three

Ben with Torre Tyson. For the 1996 baseball season and part of 1997, we were "host family" for Torre as he played for the Rochester Honkers. Torre's father, Mike, played second base and shortstop for the St. Louis Cardinals (1972-79) and Chicago Cubs (1980-81). Torre married Jennifer Adams, whose father, Tony, was the strike- replacement quarterback for the Minnesota Vikings in 1987.

years with the Minnesota Twins) joked, "Where in the world did Ransom get all that power?"

Take Me Out to the Ball Game
My aunt Bonnie and uncle Dick Forzano treated us royally when we visited them in East Liverpool, Ohio. Uncle Dick owned and managed the Traveler's Hotel, and, using his connections, he was able to get us baseball tickets. My first game seen in person was at Cleveland Stadium in the 1950s when the Indians played the New York Yankees. Cleveland is about a hundred miles from East Liverpool. Dad grew up rooting for the Yankees and remained a Yankee (and Twins) fan his entire life. I remember 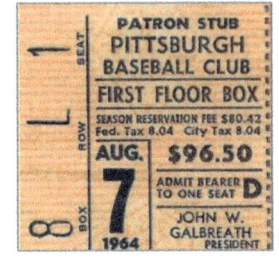 looking out at the field and feeling the excitement of seeing Mickey Mantle and the Bronx Bombers in person. The Pirates stadium, Forbes Field, was only forty miles from East Liverpool, so we attended games there several times we visited the Forzanos. On August 7, 1964, I caught a towering foul ball off the bat of Chicago Cubs third baseman Ron Santo. (Santo was inducted into the Baseball Hall of Fame in 2012.) We had just settled into our seats along the first-base line when it happened. Several seats beside us were empty, so I was able to drift down the row and smother the ball in my glove. Isn't it funny how catching a little round ball can create such a lasting memory? A year or two later, we watched Sandy Koufax *and* Don Drysdale pitch a doubleheader against the Pirates. Though the Dodgers lost both games, another baseball dream came true.

Since going to the games in Cleveland and Pittsburgh, I've attended hundreds of others (many with Jeanine): college (Iowa State University, University of Iowa, and University of Missouri), Rochester (Aces and Honkers), minor leagues (Cedar Rapids Kernels, Quad Cities River Bandits, Iowa Cubs, Portland [Maine] Sea Dogs, Scottsdale [Arizona] Firebirds, and St. Paul Saints), spring training camps (Florida and Arizona), and major leagues (in addition to the Cleveland Indians at Cleveland Stadium and the Pirates at Forbes Field there were the Twins at Met Stadium/Metrodome/Target Field, Los Angeles Dodgers at Chavez Ravine, Kansas City Royals at Kauffman Stadium,

THE OLDER I GET THE BETTER I WAS

Milwaukee Brewers at Milwaukee County Stadium, California Angels at Anaheim Stadium, San Diego Padres at Jack Murphy Stadium, St. Louis Cardinals at Busch Memorial Stadium, Pittsburgh Pirates at Three Rivers Stadium and PNC Park, Chicago Cubs at Wrigley Field, and Boston Red Sox at Fenway Park). I've been fortunate to attend the 1985 All-Star Game, several Twins postseason playoff games at the Metrodome and Target Field, and the second game of the 1987 Twins versus St. Louis Cardinals World Series, which the Twins won 8–4.

The Twins moved to Metropolitan (Met) Stadium in Bloomington in 1961. I was twelve and in junior high. I remember our baseball team busing to Knothole Day games (where kids got a ticket, hot dog, and Coke for a few dollars). Through the years, I went with family, friends, and relatives to a handful of games each season. I remember that we would usually arrive early to watch batting and infield practice. Years ago, there was an Old-Timers game that was held before a game or two a season. In those days, there were also many more scheduled doubleheaders than there are now. There's something about going to a game on a beautiful summer afternoon or evening played on a perfectly manicured diamond that used to take my breath away and still does, and I hope it always will. The grounds crew drags the infield, puts down clean white bases, and chalks the batting box and base lines. Each person knows exactly what to do and when, as if choreographed. The players lazily play pepper and catch. They joke, gaze up into the stands, smile, stretch, and jog. You meet your game family, the fans who will surround you where you're sitting. Who's there to cheer for the other team? Who's the most loyal and knowledgeable fan? Which one will be drunk by the sixth inning?

19

Which one will be the obnoxious loudmouth, hollering the same stupid thing over and over? Will anyone keep score (a lost art)? We hold our hats over our hearts, sing the National Anthem, and then Play Ball!

With my baseball idol, Sandy Koufax, during the L.A. Dodgers spring training season in Vero Beach, Florida. While I was walking to the baseball diamonds, a sports bag on my shoulder, a young boy (thinking I was a baseball player) came up to me and asked for my autograph. He made my day!

I would be remiss if I did not note that Jeanine is an even bigger baseball fan than I. She grew up idolizing players on the St. Mary's Winona college team. She and her mom attended many games. The team manager, Max Molock, let Jeanine (age twelve) ride on the tractor with him when he dragged the field. Dick Hauser played on the Winona A's minor league team in Gabrych Park. Hauser was Jeanine's

Jeanine with Baltimore Orioles pitcher Jim Palmer after a spring training game in Florida

favorite player; he would go on to play for the Kansas City Athletics and manage the Kansas City Royals. Jeanine "knew" baseball, had her own glove, and became a good slow-pitch softball player. (She was a true lefty, batting and throwing from the left side.) Jeanine was also a collector of baseball cards; we merged our collections shortly after we were married.

Harry and Jackie Bovaird were good friends of my parents. I (and Jeanine after we were married) went to many Twins baseball games with them at Met Stadium and the Metrodome. Harry and Dad both loved baseball and enjoyed a good joke. In their later years (Harry lived to eighty-seven and Dad to ninety-three) they especially loved this one:

Two old men, Carl and Kenny, have been best friends for years, they played baseball together in their youth, and they still love the game. They both live to their early nineties when Carl suddenly falls deathly ill. Kenny comes to visit him on his deathbed, and they begin reminiscing about their long friendship and how much they love baseball. Kenny says, "Listen, Carl, when you die, please do me a favor. I have always wondered if there's baseball in heaven. Can you let me know?"

Carl responds, "We've been friends for a lifetime, so yes, I'll do this for you." And a few days later he dies.

Shortly after Carl's funeral, Kenny is sleeping when he is awakened by Carl's voice. "Kenny, it's me, Carl. I've got some good news and some bad news for you. The good news is there's baseball in heaven."

"Oh, that is wonderful," says Kenny, "what could possibly be the bad news?

"You're pitching tomorrow!"

Ping Pong
Father, son, and lots of hollering

Playing ping pong with Dad in the basement of our home in 1979

Serious players call the game table tennis; we called it ping pong. I learned to play in the basement of my grandparents' farmhouse on a table my uncle Ross made in his high school shop class. When I began, probably at age seven or eight, I played with Dad, Ross, my sister, and my cousins. There wasn't much room on three sides of the table, but one end was open to the part of the basement that contained the furnace, sink, and clothes washing area. We loved the game so much that Dad put a ping pong table in the basement of our new house as it was being built. We played while construction went on above us.

Dad didn't provide much instruction. Rather, we just played and had fun. He was patient, and I got better. Our rallies grew longer and more intense from year to year. I remember the thrill of winning my first game against him. Some winter nights, a few of Dad's friends would stop by for serious singles and doubles games. The same group that played at the farm played, too, year round during family gatherings at our house. When I'd come home for weekends or holidays from college, not long after I walked in the door, Dad and I would head to the basement for a few games. I wish I would have filmed or tape-recorded a session.

Ping pong with some of Dad's friends. (Note the cigarette and mixed drink.) I'm in eighth grade and pleased they would let me play.

We usually played best out of five. We would be grunting, hollering, laughing, and then dripping with sweat from the intense workout when we'd come upstairs, sit at the kitchen table, cool down, and talk with Mom and my sister, Sue.

Dad honed his ping-pong skills playing in the service, probably in both World War II and Korea. He had a wicked backhand and would

THE OLDER I GET THE BETTER I WAS

Ping pong by the pool with Dad. We're visiting my sister, Sue, in Huntington Beach, California, 1980.

hit the ball so hard it seemed to disappear. His forehand wasn't bad, either. I had a respectable forehand and a below-average backhand; I kept up with Dad because of my quickness and ability to keep the ball in play. He sometimes would get me running from side to side—first a cross-court forehand to my forehand that I would lunge for and return—then he'd hit one to my backhand, so I'd stretch far to my left to return that one. After many rallies we were breathless from exertion and laughing so hard. I can see us looking at each other in amazement and admiration from a rally just played. I was a "thigh slapper" with my paddle. I'd often smack it in frustration if I missed a shot that ended a long rally. So, amid the grunts, shouts, and laughs, there'd be the slap, slap of rubber-coated paddle on pants leg. In the thousands of games we played, I never heard Dad swear (nor did he hear me), we never argued or disputed a call, and we never left the table mad at one another.

The ping-pong tradition continued after I moved to Rochester. We had a table at our homes on Schmidt Court and in Bamberwood. Ben and I continued the tradition of Ransom father/son matches. We had some spirited games, too, with Mark, Peter, and John Noseworthy.

Dad's skills stayed sharp late into his life. I made the following note in my journal February 3, 1980:

> Mom and Dad visited us in Rochester. Dad waxed me in ping pong. I can't figure out how he stays so good. He's 57; I'm 32. I hope he beats me forever because it has to make him feel young.

I don't recall when Dad and I stopped playing ping pong. It would have been a sad moment in our past, so it's best not to know the exact date, somewhat like the date when he grew too old to drive by himself from Clear Lake to Rochester. I have a list of things that I'd like to be able to do again if I were magically granted the chance. A best-out-of-five-games match with Dad in the basement of our Clear Lake home—when I would be about twenty (junior in college) and he forty-five—is near the top.

Volleyball
Too tired for amorous adventures

In the early 1970s, our Rochester YMCA volleyball team played the Mason City team. I'm attempting to block one of Dad's spikes.

MIKE RANSOM

I thank the Mason City YMCA for introducing Dad and me to volleyball. We moved to our new house at 1105 8th Avenue Court South in Clear Lake as I began junior high. Our junior high principal, Claude Whitehill, his wife, Wanda, and their several children lived next door. Claude was a member of the YMCA in Mason City, and he invited Dad and me to join him on many visits. Because we had so much fun, Dad bought a membership, and we began going there about once a week through the fall, winter, and spring. I don't recall us going much in the summer. We could take guests, so often we would bring Steve Sorensen, Bill Farnan, Joe Jensen, and other friends. We swam in the pool and played basketball and handball. It was much fun. In my freshman or sophomore year of high school, Dad and I started playing volleyball with the YMCA team. I recall we practiced every Wednesday night and played in tournaments. I was the only high school kid in the group; all the rest were older professionals. Because of my quickness and pretty good eye–hand coordination, I picked up on the game right away. Dad did, too. At 6 feet 2 inches, he was one of the spikers on the team. He had played volleyball in the military and had earned the nickname "Springs." At 5 feet 8 inches, I was the obvious choice to be the setter. Players I remember were Jim Brown (attorney), Darrel Bramhall, Bob (Doc) Powell (psychiatrist), John Rude, Bob Stone (Congregational Church minister), Dick Meunier, Roger Patton (attorney), Max Sowers, Howard Gorman, Bill Otterman (head of Opportunity Village in Clear Lake), John Welch (teacher), Mel Fromm (Lutheran pastor), Art Scherer (McDonalds manager), and Glen Haydon (Red Cross executive).

It was on our way to a volleyball practice in December of 1965 that Dad and I were run into head-on by another car west of Mason City on a four-lane, undivided road that was as slick as glass. We were going maybe thirty and wearing seatbelts. The force of the impact threw me forward. I couldn't get my hands up in time; my head hit the metal dash of our 1970 Chevrolet (made a small dent in it), and I popped back up with broken glasses and a badly cut, bloodied face. Dad braced his arms against the steering wheel before the impact, and they were sore for days afterward. I was taken to Mason City Mercy Hospital, just a few blocks from the accident, where my wounds were cleaned and stitched. Dad recalls that when the doctor was done, I said to him, "Let's get out of here." I had had enough of the place. My letter jacket was splotched with blood; fortunately, the dry cleaners made it look as good as new. My uncle Harlan Johnson drove Dad and me home. I believe he had called Mom to tell her that we had been in an accident, so she knew the news, but she didn't know how badly I was bloodied and bruised. It took weeks for my two black eyes and swollen nose to return to normal. I looked like a raccoon.

Dad and I looked forward to every practice and tournament with the team. They kidded me, they accepted me, and they were impressed with my setting, digging, diving, and overall hustle. We had a tournament in Sioux Falls, South Dakota, one winter weekend. Glen Haydon shared a motel room with Dad and me. Glen was fun to be around and had quite a sense of humor. As we were getting ready to turn out the lights, he started laughing uncontrollably. He had opened a desk drawer and found a *Playboy* or some other "girlie" magazine that had been left in the room. Glen and Dad joked about that for many years. I was old enough to know what they'd found, but embarrassed, too.

One of the first things I did after moving to Rochester in 1970 was join its YMCA. It had a traveling volleyball team that I became a member of and played with for several years. In April 1972, the Mason City YMCA team asked me to play with them (and Dad) in the state tournament at Ottumwa, Iowa. Jeanine came along, too. (We had recently been engaged.) Starting at 3:30 Saturday morning, Jeanine and I drove the 255 miles to Ottumwa from Rochester and arrived in time for our opening 9:30 AM game. Our team finished second overall in the tournament after playing nineteen games, our final one at 10:30 PM. Dad and I slept in one of the motel's double beds and Jeanine in the other. My legs began cramping in the middle of the night. Lying on the hard surface of the carpeted floor seemed to help, so I grabbed my pillow and a blanket and stretched out at the foot of the bed. Dad woke up in the night, realized I wasn't in bed, and thought, "Oh, oh … Mike's over there with Jeanine." He said he was afraid to look. To his surprise and relief, though, he saw me stretched out on the floor, much too exhausted for any amorous adventures. He loved talking about that tournament and motel room time for many a year.

IBM League Volleyball

Given my love of sports, the IBM intramural leagues were perfect for me. As soon as I arrived in June 1970, I played on a softball team; in the fall, I played on a championship football team; and in the winter, I began playing with excellent players on equally excellent teams in the volleyball league. In the 1970s we played our games at the Armory on North Broadway. (It became the Senior Center and is now the Castle.) We won the league championships in 1973, 1975, and 1977. My fellow team members were, in 1973, Arlen Bowen, Dick Dee, Tim Long, Ron Quandt, Chuck Sanetra, Dick Smith, Myron Snesrud, and George Thompson; in 1975, Jim Gilkinson, Fred Huss, Ron Quandt, Pete Valesano, and Emmett Woolfolk; and in 1977, Steve Dahlby, Ron Fess, Ken Hendrickson, D. E. Lloyd, Warren Wong, and Emmett Woolfolk.

In 1974 I played on an all-IBM team that was runner-up in the annual State Park and Recreation Power Volleyball Tournament held in Roseville, Minnesota, on April 6.

Our team finished second in the State Park and Recreation Volleyball Tournament. Front row: Arlen Bowen, George Thompson, Roger Kleinschmidt, Chuck Sanetra. Back row: Ed Schneider, John Earhart, Steve Speth, Jim Dillinger, and me.

THE OLDER I GET THE BETTER I WAS

Rochester YMCA Volleyball Team

Our Rochester YMCA Varsity Volleyball Team practiced at the Y every Wednesday evening. After practice, we'd amble across the street to the VFW for a pitcher or two of refreshment. We hosted an annual tournament at the Rochester Y (the Wild Goose Tournament) and traveled several weekends a winter for tournaments in Red Wing, Winona, Wausau (Wisconsin), and Mason City. As I'd been on the Mason City Y's team, I was our setter, the team's quarterback. Steve Speth was the Y's athletic director at the time. He was about 5 feet 11 inches but could jump a mile high and hammer the ball. Speth was our coach, but Arlen Bowen, with whom I also played softball, was our fiery leader. I loved setting the ball for him and our other "big guys" and hearing the loud SLAP of their powerful spikes.

Volleyball tournament at the YMCA. Jeanine and her friend Lois Graif watch from the sidelines.

Our team played some impressive volleyball. For example, on March 11, 1972, we came out on top in the ten-team St. Paul Athletic Club Invitational, defeating Red Wing in the finals. (Two weeks earlier, we had lost to Red Wing in the finals of their invitational tournament.) Our team members included Glen Edgington, Chuck Sanetra, Arlen Bowen, George Thompson, Ken Willkomm, Pat Harris, and me. After another two weeks, with the same lineup, we won the Rochester Invitational Tournament, again defeating Red Wing in the finals 16–14 and 15–6. We closed out the tournament by winning fifteen of our last sixteen games.

In the 1970s, our Rochester YMCA team traveled to the Mason City Y to play against their team. (Dad still played with them.) George Thompson was a friend and team member. He brought his two boys, Darrel and George (probably ages five and four), to the tournament. We have a Super 8 video of the tournament action that includes a shot of the boys sitting on Jeanine's lap on the sidelines. Darrel went on to play running back for the U of M football team (and still holds the yards-gained record) and then played five years for the Green Bay Packers. George played volleyball for Pepperdine University. Regarding the video of our competition: Dad asked a friend to film the action. When it came back, we realized he hadn't had much practice filming sports events. Rather than keep the camera still and let the action happen, he followed the volleyball, so after a few minutes one got seasick trying to watch us play.

5' 8" tall and born to set

At the Wild Goose Tournament on February 7, 1976, I sprained my ankle badly when Glen Lybarger and I jumped side by side to attempt to block a spike. I came down with my left foot on top of Glen's foot and fell immediately to the floor. I went to the emergency room for x-rays (it wasn't broken) and hobbled around on crutches for days. For all the running, jumping, and diving I've done in sporting activities, this sprain and a broken little finger playing basketball were my only two injuries that needed medical attention.

I set up volleyball courts in the yards of our homes on Forest Hills Drive and Schmidt Court in Rochester. Arlen Bowen had a court in his yard, too. We had many a volleyball party with family and friends (Bowen, Gilkinson, Fess, Winkle, Huss, Willkomm, and many more).

THE OLDER I GET THE BETTER I WAS

Volleyball tournament action. Here I'm sending a back set to the spiker behind me.

Volleyball in the sand is an excellent workout, especially for a two-man team. IBM added a sand volleyball court near its softball diamonds. I played many a game covered with sand after all my diving. Beach volleyball is fun, too. One spring we vacationed in Florida, primarily to golf and watch spring training baseball, but while there we had the occasion to meet up with some Rochester friends. The beach by our hotel had a few sand volleyball courts, and we were playing on them amongst ourselves when a group of guys asked if we wanted a game. We may not have looked too imposing, but we knew how to play. Jim Gilkinson and I played on the YMCA team. Rod and Sharon Morlock's daughters (Heidi and Kasey) played on the Stewartville team (and were state champions for several years) and were also outstanding basketball players. Greg Caucutt and Keith Fisher were excellent athletes. We cleaned their clocks.

Though I loved playing basketball, I did not feel I was good enough to try out for our high school team. I wish that boys' volleyball had been an option. I think I could have made the team, contributed, and had lots of fun. Some high schools have begun offering the sport to boys, which I commend them for doing.

Slow-Pitch Softball

They called me "Wheels."

Beating out an infield hit at a softball tournament in the early 1970s

MIKE RANSOM

Soon after joining IBM in 1970 as a technical writer, I was asked to play on a slow-pitch softball team called Charlie Brown's All Stars. We practiced and played league games on a softball diamond near the barn in the IBM park. (IBM stored computer equipment and supplies in the barn.) The diamond was dug up and the barn torn down many years ago and replaced with tennis courts. We were a rag-tag, play-for-fun kind of team. Larry Collins, one of the technical writing managers, was on the team, and I probably got my invitation to join from him. Other members I can recall were Greg Caucutt, Dave Hoffman, Jim Sloan, Ron King, Ron Madden, Harlan Gerke, and Henry Kemp. We weren't too good. In 1971 we got beat 46–2 by a powerhouse team that had many first-rate players (Rod Morlock, Ben Borgen, and others).

By 1973 I had moved on to teams with much better players and leagues with much better teams. That year I played second base on a team that won the IBM Club Championship. Team members were Ben Borgen, Arlen Bowen, Jim Hendrick, Gene Jorgensen, Dave Linnerooth, Tim Long, Merlin Malde, Rod Morlock, John Roemer, Chuck Sanetra, G. F. Snyder, Dick Weltzin, and Morry Witter. The following year, 1974, we were Tuesday League champions. My fellow teammates were Brian Bjerke, Ben Borgen, Arlen Bowen, Jim Hendrick, G. A. Fischer, Gene Jorgensen, Dave Linnerooth, Murlin Miller, Rod Morlock, John Roemer, and Morry Witter. For both of these years, I played with several of the IBM team members in the Rochester city slow-pitch league.

I was a pretty good infielder. I loved to dive for balls to my left and right. During one IBM league game when I was playing shortstop, I remember a slow roller that was hit to me. I raced forward, picked it up bare-handed, and threw it in one motion while I ended up diving and landing on my stomach. Got the runner out by an eyelash. Another time, again in the IBM league, I was playing third base, which I rarely did. We played a team that Gordy Bishop captained. Gordy was an intense competitor. I think he hit three smashes at me during the game, and I got him out on each. During one of his at bats there were runners on first and second and one out, and he hit a hot one at me. I fielded it, stepped on third for an out, and then fired to first to double him up.

THE OLDER I GET THE BETTER I WAS

In addition to IBM intramural softball, I competed in the top city softball league, which had six to eight teams made up of outstanding players. Games were played through the summer two nights a week (probably Tuesdays and Thursdays) on the Soldiers Field diamonds to the north of the golf course and swimming pool. There were two games, early (around 6:00) and late (around 8:00), on each diamond. Games were wonderfully intense.

Jim & Joe's was the team to beat. Two players on their team, shortstop Les Ernster and second baseman Dave Dostal, were inducted into the Minnesota State Softball Hall of Fame. (Jon Springer, who umpired our games for many years, was also inducted into the State Softball Hall of Fame.)

Teams on which I played were Clark's Super 100 from 1971 to 1972, Postier Pump from 1973 to 1975 (we had basically the same players, just changed sponsors), and Golden George's from 1976 to 1979. All three teams played in the top league in Rochester. Teams I played on would also compete in a few weekend tournaments in surrounding towns (Alma, Wisconsin, for example) each summer with ten, twenty, or more high-caliber teams.

The Clark's Super 100 players were Morry Witter (pitcher), Rod Morlock (catcher), Clark Marshall (first base), me (second base), Dave Linnerooth and Tim Long (third base), Gene Jorgensen (shortstop), Ben Borgen (left field), John Roemer (left center field), Merlin Malde (right center field), and Arlen Bowen (right field). In 1971 we lost to Jim & Joe's 23–13, 3–2, and 23–6 during the season. In the end-of-season playoffs we lost the first game 11–8, won the second 10–9, and then fell in the championship game 7–6 in eight innings. In 1972, we finished the season with sixteen wins and seven losses, including season losses to Jim & Joe's of 15–1 and 6–5. We lost in the playoffs to them 8–4 and 12–1.

The Postier Pump players and positions were nearly the same as our Clark's Super 100 Team, except that Dave Postier played left center field. We finished first in the Rochester City league with a record of 12–5 and beat Lobster House, managed by Gordy Bishop, in the playoffs 6–4 and 5–1 to go to the state tournament in Coon Rapids. We beat St. Cloud 17–2 before losing to Chaska 7–4 on an umpire's bad call. Jim & Joe's was not in the league that year. Dave Linnerooth

37

managed our team. Managers of other teams in the league were Rod Toomey, Bill Beaupre, Barry Woodle, Gordy Bishop, and Jack Lampman. In 1974, when Jim & Joe's was back in the league, we finished third overall with a 12–11 record. We lost to Jim & Joe's 11–3, 8–4, and 12–4 during the season. The Hollywood Lounge team, managed by Buzz Hanson, won the playoffs and went to State. We won fourteen and lost seven in 1975, finished first in the regular season (despite losses to Jim & Joe's of 7–3, 8–6, and 4–0), won the playoffs, and went to the state tournament, where we didn't do well.

Jeanine's ticket for watching our slow-pitch softball state tournament games

The Golden George's team I played on had the following players: Gary Murray (pitcher), Barry Woodle (catcher), Bruce Almy and Al Larson (first base), me (second base), Jim Harens (third base), Jim Mickelson (shortstop), Gary Allar (left field), Lee Sandstrom (left center field), Murlin Miller (right center field), and Arlen Bowen (right field).

Rather than a baseball cap, I usually wore a headband. That's why Arlen Bowen started calling me "Hippie." Arlen was a challenging teammate. He and I were (and are) good friends, but boy did he have a temper. If looks could kill, when he got angry, he could have put away the entire team. He played right field. One game, I did something particularly stupid at second base. We were on the east field. Arlen got so mad that he hollered at me and then threw his glove over the right-field fence. The umpire called time while Arlen lumbered around the fence to retrieve it.

I can still see turning a double play with shortstop Gene Jorgensen. I made sure to get to the bag early because Gene had a quick release and fired the ball to me extra hard. I had to be ready so I could catch, turn, and throw to first and avoid the runner barreling in to second base trying to disrupt things.

Morry Witter was an excellent pitcher. He was older than the rest of the guys on the team and worked for the IBM credit union. He was somewhat stocky and didn't look like an athlete, but could he pitch and hit. His pitches had a high arc that crossed the back of the plate. At bat, he masterfully placed the ball to any open area of the outfield with an easy, fluid swing. He didn't ever flail at a pitch; he made hitting look so effortless.

Ben Borgen in left field had a cannon for an arm. On a ball hit his way where the runner might be thinking of stretching a single into a double, Ben would field it and fire it to me on a rope. The ball would first dip down low, almost clip the grass, and then rise a foot or more as it came to me at second base. It was frightening at times, especially when the ball and the runner were arriving simultaneously. I had to keep an eye on a ball that could maim me if I missed it *and* a runner intent on knocking me over.

In all of my youth and high school baseball games and then slow-pitch softball games, I never came close to hitting an over-the-fence home run. I was a slap, spray, and line-drive hitter who batted lead-off and, with my speed, made things happen. I can still hear the other team hollering "Wheels!" when I would come up to bat; it was their signal to one another to be on their toes and hustle their throws to first because I beat out a lot of infield ground balls.

There was something special about the excitement of getting ready for a league game on warm summer nights or before a tournament game on weekends. Stretching, running sprints, and playing catch to loosen up. The smack of the ball in my glove. The good feeling of being able to throw hard on target. The pristine ball diamond with its smooth dirt, white chalk lines, clean bases, and freshly mown outfield grass. An excitement like none other.

The winter of 1970, I broke my right-hand little finger in a YMCA basketball game. I was trying to save a basketball from going back over midcourt. I reached, grabbed it, and when I flung it backward, my hand hit my knee and broke my finger. Off I went to the emergency room for surgery by Dr. Linsheid. Pins and everything. After my finger healed, before every softball game (and almost all other sports I played), I would tape it to the one next to it with white athletic tape to protect it from reinjury. The tape got sweat soaked and dirty as the game went along. Fortunately, my taped fingers didn't seem to bother my fielding, throwing accuracy, or hitting.

On the weekend of June 19 and 20 in 1976, I played for a team called the Beaver Hawks in a tournament in Spring Valley. Greg Caucutt and I were asked to fill in for some players who couldn't be there that weekend. Dick Estry played center field; Steve Dahlby played first base. I can't remember the rest of the lineup. We lost our first game and then won the next five. I played second base, fielded well, and hit the heck out of the ball for the whole tournament (maybe eighteen for twenty-four). I was worn out from running the bases. We played a team made up of Rochester Community College football players and their coach, Cy Champa. I remember one huge, left-handed batter (probably a lineman) who killed the ball my way each time up, and I got him out with some outstanding fielding plays. Our team of littler, faster players had them shaking their heads. It was one of those games when you're so in the groove that you want every ball to be hit to you. It's those moments you live for.

From a playing perspective, I enjoyed softball as much as I did baseball. My grandpa Ransom played a variation of softball called kitten ball, and Dad played fast-pitch and slow-pitch softball, so I was pleased to carry on the Ransom softball tradition.

Football

Lamar Hunt and I watch his Kansas City Chiefs.

With Kansas City Chiefs owner Lamar Hunt after he and I jogged around the Chiefs' Arrowhead Stadium

Ollie Matson came into the National Football League in 1952 as a running back and receiver for the Chicago Cardinals, was traded to the Los Angeles Rams following the 1958 season, and was elected to the Pro Football Hall of Fame in 1972. I'm not sure how or why I became a fan of his. It may have been from his football card. I had quite a few of these cards, though not nearly as many as in my baseball card collection. When I was eight or nine, I would take a few of Mom's and Dad's poker chips, pretend each was a football player, and roll them (run plays) on the "football field" that ran goal line to goal line from the living room into the kitchen of our house. Ollie was my favorite player, and he executed one dazzling poker-chip run after another. I would scoot along on the tile floor rolling the chips for hours on end.

About that time, I began to take a keen interest in the University of Iowa Hawkeyes football team. Their games were broadcast on radio, and I hung on every word of the announcer's play-by-play action. The Hawkeyes had outstanding teams back then. Players I idolized included Kenny Ploen, Randy Duncan, Bob Jeter, Willie Fleming, and Alex Karras. Iowa went to the Rose Bowl (in Pasadena, California) in 1957, played Oregon State, and won by a score of 35–19. They raced out to a 14–0 lead behind quarterback Kenny Ploen, the Rose Bowl MVP. He ran for a forty-nine–yard touchdown to open the scoring and connected on nine of ten passes. Rambunctious Iowa fans ripped down the goalposts at one end of the Rose Bowl field with four seconds still left on the clock. The Hawkeyes returned to the Rose Bowl in 1959, this time beating California 38–12. The Hawks smashed four Rose Bowl offensive records, including four hundred and twenty-nine yards for rushing. Iowa led 20–0 at halftime and piled it on in the third quarter when Willie Fleming and Bob Jeter broke loose for touchdown runs of thirty-seven and eighty-one yards, respectively.

I remember on New Year's Day visiting Grandma and Grandpa at their farm. The Rose Bowl game was televised, but the reception on their TV was so snowy it looked like the game was being played in a raging blizzard. No matter which way we turned the TV's rabbit ears, the reception was terrible. But we didn't care; our beloved Hawkeyes were playing in the Rose Bowl. How exciting!

Many Iowa Hawkeye players—Jerry Reichow, Alex Karras, and Jim Gibbons to name a few—went on to play for the Detroit Lions in the NFL, so I became a Lions fan prior to the Vikings coming to Minnesota.

Though I had a strong throwing arm in baseball, I could never throw a football with any zip on it. I could, however, catch and punt with the best. Dad and I would go out in the back yard on cool fall days. I would hike the ball to him and run various pass routes, and he would rifle the ball to me. Then we'd punt. He'd stand in the alley near the Eastman's two-story garage. (Don Eastman drove large grain trucks and parked the cabs inside.) I would be opposite him in our neighbor's (Bob and Irene Nichols) backyard. We would kick our white-with-black-stripes, leather football back and forth. I loved punting, and still do even today. When Ben and I punt the ball back and forth in our yard in Bamberwood, it reminds me of days doing the same with Dad. He and I would also pass and kick in front of the barn and milk house at Grandpa and Grandma's farm. I would start my routes parallel to the row of lilac trees and then cut over the middle to catch passes.

Starting in fifth or sixth grade and continuing through my freshman or sophomore year in high school, I played touch football with friends in the open field by the Lincoln School playground. Many Saturday and Sunday afternoons in the fall I biked there to play pickup games for hours. Friends who played included Steve Sorensen, Lloyd Batchelor, Gary Lamping, Tim Sill, Bob Calhoun, Dick Calhoun, Mark Schoneman, Jim Larsen, and Dave Erickson. We were all pretty good athletes and played some exciting games. Steve had a tremendous passing arm. I made some dazzling catches, ran punts and kickoffs back for touchdowns, and punted, too. Of the dozens—if not hundreds—

of games we played, I don't recall anyone getting hurt, arguing, or going home mad, nor do I ever recall a parent stopping by to watch us play. I would bike home dog tired as the late afternoon darkness crept in, and if it were Sunday, sorry the weekend was ending and that I'd need to get ready for school the next morning.

As much as I loved touch football, I couldn't bring myself to play tackle. Because of my speed and quickness, the coaches asked me to try out. (I remember assistant football coach Mr. [Richard] Hudson twisting my arm.) The team's head coach, Gus Brandt, also coached baseball, my true sports love. In Mr. Brandt's math classroom, he sometimes watched films of the team's football games on a projector. In hindsight, I'm glad I didn't play high school tackle football. Who knows what ankle, leg, hip, and head injuries I might have had? I maybe could have made the team as their punter, but I'm not sure if they were that specialized back then. Many players played both ways—offense and defense—so just punting would have been kind of "wimpy." My only on-field experiences came during home games as a member of the high school marching band. I played bass clarinet. One fall night I remember us lined up on the field in formation, ready to play the "Star-Spangled Banner." Ludwig (Lud) Wangberg, our marching and concert band director, raised his baton, got our attention, and started us playing. Musical disaster ensued. We were obviously seriously out of sync and past the point of recovery. Lud stopped us, glared, and gave another downbeat of his baton for us to begin again. He took music seriously. When frustrated or angry, his face would turn crimson, and he looked ready to explode. It's good he stopped us when he did. The restart went well.

Our hometown newspaper, *The Clear Lake Mirror Report*, sponsored a football contest during the fall. The Wednesday weekly edition contained a form that listed about thirty high school and college football games to be played the Friday and Saturday of the week. Contestants selected a winner for each game and for one designated game, guessed the points total for the two teams. Those points would be used to determine winners in case of ties. Rules were that a person could submit only one entry. Dad and I looked forward each week to the contest and would round up extra copies of the form so that we could fill out one ourselves and for other family members. The Ransoms made headlines in October 1965 when four of us (Dad, Sue, Grandpa Ransom, and I) finished first, second, third, and fourth. The prizes were nominal, I'm sure, but we were as excited as if we had won the Powerball lottery.

Ransoms Sweep Football Contest

Oct 27 1965

The football contest this week turned into a family affair, the first four places went to members of the Ransom family. First place was taken by Mike Ransom with 24 correct picks. Second place went to James A. Ransom with 24 correct picks Mike was six points closer on the tie breaker. They both live at 1105 8th Ave. Ct. South. Third place also with 24 correct was James H. Ransom of Rural Route 1. He was nine points farther away on the tie breaker than Mike. Another Ransom, Sue, also had 24 correct picks but was eliminated from the top three by the tie breaker.

The toughies this week were the Iowa-Northwestern game and the upset of Texas by Rice Institute.

This was the largest response we've had to the contest this season, also there appeared to be a great deal of study put into the selections, because the correct picks were high this week.

We received an entry without a name this week, so again we caution you to make sure you put your name and address on your entry.

Our family's football contest claim to fame

In the fall of 1970, just months after I joined IBM, I was asked to play on one of their intramural touch football teams. IBM's teams and leagues were top-notch, loaded with outstanding athletes. Jim Harens (who had offered me the IBM job) was our quarterback, and several others on the team were friends I had met in my first few months at work: Greg Caucutt, Gary Allar, Jerry Will, and more. (At Michigan State University, Greg played on a football team that won the university intramural title. He said, "I got on Mike Marshall's team; he was a legendary intramural quarterback. When he turned pro, the university declared him ineligible to play any intramurals." Marshall ended up playing from 1967 through 1981 for nine different MLB teams. He won the National League Cy Young Award in 1974, when he pitched for the L.A. Dodgers, and was a two-time All-Star selection.)

There were seven or eight teams in the league, and we played once a week in the fall. I recall playing defensive back and wide receiver for our team, captained by Harens. The team to beat in the league was captained by Jerry Knutson. Rod Morlock and Ben Borgen played on the Knutson team. Each fall they would check the new IBM hires and try to recruit the best athletes for their team. They usually succeeded in doing so, and their records showed it.

Knutson's team opened the year with a surprise tie with an underdog team captained by Tom Crooks. Our Harens team beat Knutson's team 20–7 and won all the rest of our games up until the last regular season game, which we lost to Led Davis's team 20–7. Knutson had beaten Davis during the season, so the only blemishes on the Knutson record were their loss to us and their tie with Crooks. At the end of the regular season, our team and Davis's team were tied with one loss and qualified to play in the league championship game. Knutson's team, with one loss and a tie, didn't make the top two.

We won the championship game with a come-from-behind victory on a Saturday morning. The Davis team had a 12–0 lead with two minutes left in the game. Greg Caucutt caught a fourth-down bomb from Harens for a touchdown because Dennis Bassett, who was all over him, mistimed his jump and the ball fell into Greg's hands. Led Davis was an athletic quarterback. His team should have had the game in the bag; they just needed to run out the clock after receiving our kickoff. On their first play, rather than hand the ball off, Led took the snap and started to run around in the backfield, faking a pass. Jerry Will knocked the ball out of Led's hands and caught it, so we had the ball back with time for a play. We got a touchdown and an extra point to win as time ran out. There was quite a celebration afterward at the North Star Bar on Broadway. My friend from Clear Lake, Bill Farnan, was home on leave from Army basic training visiting Steve Sorensen and me for the weekend. We three left after the game rather than joining in the team's revelry, which probably saved me a serious celebration hangover.

IBM touch football league champions, 1970: Back row left to right: Gil Bean, Ron Fess, Jerry Will, Dick Skarda, Jerry Ovesen, Roger Nelson, Harold Wright, Frank Benson, John Harrington, me. Front row: Ray McRoberts, Gary Allar, Greg Caucutt, Murlin Miller, Jim Harens, Jim Cook, Chuck Stupca, Dick Estry, Gary Murray

    Sometime in the early 1970s, I remember subbing on a city league touch football team. Games were played under the lights at Soldiers Field. Though the IBM league had some big and tough players, the city league players were much bigger, stronger, and faster. I was terrified and my main goal was not to get maimed. I recall recovering a fumble on a kickoff and being relieved that I had contributed something positive to my team.

    Though Jeanine and I have seen hundreds of Twins baseball games at Met Stadium, the Metrodome, and Target Field in person, we have attended only a handful of Vikings games. One of the few games we saw (with Steve and Jennifer Sorensen) turned out to be one of the Vikings' most memorable, a heartbreaking divisional playoff loss to the Dallas Cowboys. It took place at Met Stadium on December 28, 1975. The Vikings were upset, 17-14, when the Dallas Cowboys scored on a last minute 50-yard touchdown pass from Roger Staubach to Drew Pearson. Cornerback Nate Wright, who covered Pearson on the play, contended he fell because he was pushed, and offensive interference should have been called. Dallas advanced in the playoffs to beat the Los Angeles Rams and then lost to the Pittsburgh Steelers in the Super Bowl.

New Orleans is the furthest I've traveled for a Vikings game. I went there by train in the early 1970s on a trip with IBM friends Murlin Miller, Bruce Almy, Gary Murray, and several others. Afterward, I flew to Boca Raton, Florida, for a business meeting.

Though the Vikings–Dallas playoff game at Met Stadium was memorable, the best game I will likely ever attend took place on November 17, 1991, at the Kansas City Chiefs Arrowhead Stadium. The Chiefs played the John Elway–led Denver Broncos. Dan Harris (my sister Sue's husband) was best friends with Lamar Hunt, Jr., whose father, Lamar Sr., owned the team. Jeanine, Ben, and I took Dad along and met Sue and Dan in Kansas City. The night before the game, we were invited to join the Hunts at a fancy Italian restaurant. Our group of six joined Lamar Sr., his wife, Norma, Lamar Jr. and his wife, and Clark (another of Lamar's sons) and his girlfriend (Miss Kansas at the time). Before dinner, Ben was given a private tour of the kitchen. During our over-dinner conversation, I mentioned to Lamar Sr. that I was a jogger. "Are you?" he replied. "I love jogging, too. How would you like to join me on my run in the morning before the game?" How could I say no? Lamar and Norma stayed that night at their in-stadium "home," an apartment that was connected to the owner's box. When I knocked on their door in the morning, Lamar soon appeared sporting his Kansas City Chiefs red jogging suit. It was drizzling rain, so we decided to run the covered loop around the stadium and past the concession stands. I don't recall much about the run other than (1) Lamar jogged pretty slowly (he was fifty-nine, which seemed old to me at the time) and (2) every few minutes we would pass a stadium worker or volunteer who said, "Good morning, Mr. Hunt." I bet each one of them wondered who the heck the guy jogging with him was.

THE OLDER I GET THE BETTER I WAS

What an experience to watch the game from Lamar Hunt's owner's box. There were rows of cushioned seats where guests sat and had a perfect fifty-yard-line view of the on-field action. Behind the seats were tables on which ample amounts of delicious food and drink were available. I recall the box holding forty or fifty guests. Henry Bloch (of H&R Block) was there, as were other dignitaries. I visited with the governor of Nebraska. During the game, I noticed a football championship ring the size of a walnut on the finger of the man seated next to me. Upon closer inspection, I could see that it was a ring for the San Diego Chargers win in the 1963 American Football League Championship Game and figured out I was shoulder to shoulder with Sid Gillman, one of the best offensive football minds that ever played or coached the game. As the game went on, I got up the nerve to talk to him (he was eighty at the time). I don't recall much of our conversation, but I'll always remember looking down at that ring and realizing who was wearing it.

Seventy-five thousand fans were in attendance. The game was a nail biter. Kansas City scored ten points in the second quarter to tie the Broncos 10–10 at halftime. Elway led his team to score fourteen points in the third quarter to the Chiefs' three, so it was 24–13 to start the fourth quarter. The Chiefs' starting quarterback, Steve DeBerg, had to leave the game with an injury and was replaced by Mark Vlasic, who threw a touchdown pass in the third quarter to make the score 24–20. Kansas City had the ball and was driving down field in the final minutes of the fourth quarter and needed a touchdown to win. Vlasic completed a pass near the Broncos goal line, but there was some confusion about running the next play, and time ran out. A disappointing loss for the Chiefs, but what a memorable game for the Ransoms. Lamar apologized to us at the game's end. He said, "I would liked to have taken you and Ben down to the Chiefs' locker room to meet the players, but after a loss, because I know how frustrated they are, I don't make that trip." A visit to the locker room would have been the only thing that could possibly have made the day any better than it was. Today, the Lamar Hunt Trophy is given to the winner of the AFC Championship Game in the National Football League.

I made a business trip to Houston a few weeks before Christmas in 1995. I flew first class on the way back, which I rarely did. As I settled into my seat, I heard one of the flight attendants saying to another that we were going to have a celebrity on board. Little did I know that he would be sitting right next to me. In a few minutes, in walked an immaculately dressed man who had "professional athlete" written all over him. I'm not one to quickly start up a conversation with my airplane seatmates, so I didn't say a word, but I watched him out of the corner of my eye. We were served breakfast, and I noticed that he bowed his head in prayer for a short time. Following breakfast, he pulled some letters from his briefcase and began reading them. It was then I confirmed who I thought the man was, because the letters were addressed to Warren Moon, quarterback of the Minnesota Vikings. We were traveling on a Friday, and Moon would in a few days be quarterbacking the team on a Monday Night Football Game of the Week. It was fascinating to me to be sitting next to a guy who shortly would be performing in front of millions. He didn't seem fazed by the thought at all. Moon was in the news for alleged spouse abuse. Earlier in the year he had been accused of hitting and choking his then-wife Felicia. (In February of 1996, it took less than a half hour for jurors to deliver a verdict of not guilty. Felicia stood by her husband and denied knowing how she got bruises and injuries that were shown in police photographs.) I didn't initiate any conversation with Moon during the flight, but when we landed, I asked him for a "to Ben" autograph, which he gladly provided

Football has replaced baseball as America's pastime. I have mixed feelings about the game. Players have gotten much bigger, faster, and more fearless than when I grew up. Today more and more former players are suffering early Alzheimer's and other effects of multiple concussions that come from violent collisions. I'm glad that I played only touch football and that Ben chose not to try out for his high school team.

Cross-Country Skiing
Fifty-five kilometers with 7,000 Scandinavians

Crossing the 1988 Birkebeiner finish line with Dave Ness at Telemark Lodge in Cable, Wisconsin

I started cross-country skiing somewhat late in life. A many-acres pasture behind our house in Forest Hills provided a convenient area to ski. I believe the first pairs of wooden skis and poles that Jeanine and I bought were from Tyrol Ski & Sports in Rochester. We began to ski around the pasture, on the Rochester golf courses, at Quarry Hill Nature Center, and at Clear Lake (golf course and lake). When Jeanine and I skied behind our Forest Hills home, our springer spaniel, Harley, bounded along through the snow beside us, which was often a foot or more deep. He would burrow his head into it, sniff out mice, and bark at them. We

Cross-country skiing in one of Rochester's flat, wide-open areas

laughed at his muffled barks and the pencil stub of a tail that wagged excitedly in the air. The home we built in 1978 at Schmidt Court was on three wooded acres. Our friends and neighbors Duane and Diane Ilstrup helped clear a hiking trail from our houses to the tennis court on the south end of the subdivision. In the winter, we could cross-country ski (and snowshoe) on the trail to the court and then out into the open field beyond it. Dad skied with us, too, with his big, wide, heavy bushwhacking skis. I can see him flying down a steep Quarry Hill trail with a cornfield alongside it. If he missed a turn (which he often did), he would go flying through the bent-over stalks, often balancing on one ski and laughing all the way. At the country club, there was one hill we called the "deadly triple" that began at the furthest back of the three tiered tee boxes. We picked up speed as we dropped down each one, so we had a fast start down the hill.

Jeanine and I hosted parties for friends at Schmidt Court where we first skied at Eastwood Golf Course and then came back to our house for dinner. I started skiing for workouts with Greg Caucutt, Bob

Waite, and others. We'd meet at a local golf course and ski for an hour or two. Greg and I skied at Forestville State Park, too. Two of our friends, Mike Tomashek and Henry Hocraffer, were top-tier skiers. They skate skied, which the better skiers did. I employed the classic style.

IBM friend Dave Ness and I decided, in 1988, to sign up for the American Birkebeiner (the Birkie), a fifty-five-kilometer (thirty-four-mile) race in Wisconsin, advertised as "the race that everybody wins." It started in Hayward, Wisconsin, and ended at the Telemark Lodge in Cable. (Starting in 1992, the race reversed directions, going from Cable to Hayward.) The Birkie is the largest cross-country ski race in North America, It debuted in 1973. Skiers from around the world come to the race. It has a reputation for attracting skiers of varying ability levels. Olympians and national team members have competed in the event, and it also draws recreational skiers from Wisconsin, Minnesota, and the Upper Peninsula of Michigan; neighboring Ontario, Canada; and other countries. The race weekend also includes the shorter twenty-nine-kilometer Kortelopet.

American Birkebeiner XVI
February 20, 1988

Contestants are grouped in starting waves of a thousand or more skiers each, depending on their anticipated finish times. The first wave consists of some of the best skiers in the world. Dave and I put in quite a few training miles on weekends to prepare for the race. He and I were probably in the eighth or ninth of the ten waves.

Dean Ascheman, a mutual friend, was kind enough to let us stay the night before in his lake cabin several miles from the start. Jeanine and Kathy (Dave's wife) came along for moral support. The furnace went out during the night. At three o'clock in the morning, Dave (about 6 feet 2 inches) and I (much shorter than that) were stretched out under the cabin's crawl space trying to fix the furnace. We finally got it working but lost much needed sleep in the process.

Jeanine and Kathy were at a restaurant in Hayward not far from the start of the race to cheer us on (and then moved to spots further down the trail as the day went along). Kathy filmed the skiers. Watching her film was a hoot. It begins with the world's best flying by. They are just a blur because they're going so fast. The next wave is slightly slower, and each wave continues that pattern. By the time Dave and I get to the camera, we're going so slow compared with those before us that it looks like Kathy had switched to filming in slow motion.

Dave and I finished the Birkie in seven hours and twenty-four minutes. There were about 7,000 skiers. We skied along scenic, perfectly groomed trails through woods. The temperature was five degrees, and it was windy when we began. The temp rose to twenty degrees by midday. We were so proud of our accomplishment. Neither of us fell once on the many steep hills and tricky, twisting turns. Skiers were carried off left and right on sleds pulled behind snowmobiles from falls or hypothermia. I've never attempted a running marathon (my goal in life has always been to never run one), but finishing the Birkebeiner, hiking from the North to the South Rim of the Grand Canyon, and riding multiple RAGRAIs (bike rides across Iowa) are accomplishments I feel are in the same class. Dave and I did not care what our time was; we just wanted to finish. A seventy-year-old grandmother had a faster time than we did. Tomashek and Hocraffer, probably in the wave right after the world-class skiers, were done with the race and three hours into their car ride back to Rochester (at about Zumbrota) when Dave and I crossed the finish line. It was the only full Birkebeiner I did. Dave and I skied several pre-Birkebeiners (training races held a week or two before the race) and one or more Kortelopets. I think Dave skied several full Birkebeiners.

The skating technique appealed to me, so I bought skating skis and practiced diligently. I could never quite get the hang of it to make it look as smooth, effortless, and fast as the good skiers did. One year, though, I signed up for the Kortelopet and trained to skate it. A heavy, fresh snow began to fall the February morning in 1991 when I started, and it continued through the race. I had waxed my skis for older snow; I didn't have any other type of wax, and I skied the whole way feeling like I was slogging through sand. Jeanine and Ben were there cheering me on. Our plan was for us to hop in the car right after I finished and drive to Minneapolis for a Paul Simon concert. Because I skied slower than planned and the highways to the cities were snow covered, it took us longer than it should have. We made it to Target Center just as Simon was beginning his opening song, "The Obvious Child," from his *The Rhythm of the Saints* album. I can still hear the drumbeats that opened the song and feel the excitement of being there to hear Simon and his band for a three-hour performance. I've always been glad we didn't miss that moment. An aside: The Houston Rockets NBA team was staying at our hotel. At breakfast the next morning, team members ate breakfast at tables near us. The players standing in the lobby looked like a forest of redwood trees.

I have been a recreational cross-country skier rather than a competitive one, and I'm pleased that my technique improved over the years so that skiing provided such a good overall workout. There aren't many things that top skiing on freshly groomed trails through quiet woods on a twenty-degree winter day.

Tennis
How I stopped running around my backhand.

Stroking a backhand on our Bamberwood tennis court

My first recollections of playing tennis are of warm summer nights under the lights on the Clear Lake Lions Field courts. Steve Sorensen, Lloyd Batchelor, and Jim Larsen were among the regulars who would hit the ball for hours. What a good way to spend an evening when young and carefree. After tennis, we would take off for a root beer at the Lighthouse Drive-in or motor to Mason City to drag Federal Avenue, its main street. I played some tennis in college (Iowa State had exceptional recreational facilities, including many tennis courts). I remember matches with Dave Madsen, the person who talked me into taking computer science my sophomore year when those classes were first offered. I was athletic and quick, so I could keep the ball in play and give my opponents a good run for their money. My backhand was the weak link in my game. Early on, I recall "running around it" so I could hit all returns with my forehand; that was a dead giveaway of an amateur player.

Dad and I played on the courts across the road from the Clear Lake High School. At Schmidt Court, where Jeanine and I lived from 1978 to 1986, the common area had a cement court on which we played. The white concrete was really bright and hot on sunny summer days, and the rough surface chewed up tennis balls and shoes. I can remember many weekend mornings bicycling from home the seven miles to the Outdoor Club tennis courts to play a couple hours of doubles, biking to Mr. Donut afterward to pick up a dozen donuts, and then cycling back home to have breakfast, and not thinking twice of the energy required to do so.

With Dad on Father's Day, 1978

At IBM I became friends with Jim Gilkinson, Dave Winkle, Fred Huss, and Gene Jones. These guys were "real" tennis players, and from playing with them, I (and my backhand) improved each year. I played and did relatively well in IBM intramural tournaments. Tennis was booming in Rochester in the 1970s. One would drive all over town after work and on weekends looking for an open city court—at Soldiers Field, Goose Egg Park, Mayo High School, Kutzky Park, and more. IBM eventually tore down its barn and nearby softball field and replaced them with a running track and tennis courts. The courts were popular because you could make reservations. (That was also allowed at the Outdoor and Indoor Clubs; you could make reservations and join leagues with reserved times for play. It was another reason why I joined.) We played late at night under the lights at Soldiers Field, too. Looking back on my 1970s calendars, I see that I played tennis often with Gary Allar, Greg Caucutt, and Ron Fess, coworkers at IBM.

Tennis at the Soldiers Field courts

One of the few times I remember getting mad in sports competitions happened on the Rochester Athletic Club courts. I was playing the college-aged son (I'll call him Jared) of a friend. Jared was good, played competitively, and aspired to lofty goals in tennis. We had played several times before, so this wasn't our first friendly match, but it was the first time I'd seen him be so hot headed. He was swearing and throwing his racket. When I'd seen all I could take, I walked up to the net and said, "Jared, if you can't be a better sport, we should quit." I believe he had a big lead at the time, maybe 4–1 in the set. He decided we should keep playing with the understanding that he'd straighten up. I recall playing out of my mind when we resumed and winning five games in a row. It was all he could do to contain himself as I came back from behind to win. It was one of my more satisfying victories. I don't think we ever played again.

Another time, I played a new hire in our department from "out East." He was a good guy, athletic, and confident. When we found out we had a mutual interest in tennis, I reserved a court for a match. I beat him 6–0 and 6–0. He said, "I can't believe what just happened. I've never been skunked before."

Tennis in Huntington Beach, California, 1979, while visiting my sister, Sue

Forrest Parry and Art Hamburgen were two IBM upper-level managers, probably ten or more years older than me, who were avid doubles players. They teamed up so often that you began to think Parry/Hamburgen was one person rather than two. They were talented, likeable players who competed hard and fair. Larry Osterwise (IBM Rochester General Manager at the time) and I entered an Indoor Tennis doubles tournament. In our match with Forrest and Art, I made a play that changed the momentum of a match that we eventually won, a play that Art would retell for years to come. Forrest or Art hit a soft, angled shot just over the net that landed fair but was headed out of bounds. I charged forward, either lunged or dove to reach the ball, and flicked it softly cross court, along their side of the net, where it landed out of their reach. It's funny, but as I write the story, I can see the court we were on and my going for the ball. I think I even amazed myself with that "get."

Here's a note from a doubles match I played on September 18, 1989, with three extremely good tennis players:

> Played tennis out of my mind! Subbed and played at the Indoor Club with Suresh, Ken Lawrence, and Fred Huss. Served well, hit all sorts of good shots. Great feeling. First time to play indoors this fall. Ended with my chasing down a lob and hitting backhand winning smash down the line.

With Ben and Mark and John Noseworthy. Good friends, good tennis.

To close, here's something I wrote about tennis back on June 18, 1979:

> Tennis can be extremely rewarding yet extremely frustrating. On good nights, the racket feels like part of my body. First serves fall in regularly, my backhand is reasonable, and my forehand to the backhand corner is on. Tonight, I played Dave Limpert, and it reinforced how much fun good tennis can be. When my game goes sour, it will be best to remember these good nights. Spring in the legs, good anticipation, a relaxed service return—all fall in place at times. It's nights like tonight I feel I'm capable of playing quality tennis, something I'm improving on each year. I felt in

control. I could hit the ball hard, backhand and forehand, and get it in. I played well at the net. Got low for my volleys and drop shots. Really neat feeling to play hard. When doing so, you love every minute and wish you could play forever.

Racquetball
My best sport

A photo that Rochester Post Bulletin *photographer Jerry Olson took of me playing Jim Ebbitt in the City Racquetball Tournament singles championship match*

Racquetball has been one of the sports most ideally suited to my skills and strengths—hand–eye coordination, quickness, conditioning, diving—and it's the sport in which I've ranked among the very best of all players in Rochester and made the Racquetball Hall of Fame.

Before racquetball became popular, I began playing handball at the Mason City YMCA against Dad and other men who were pretty good at the sport. The Y had only one court. I was probably a freshman in high school. During my junior and senior years in high school, paddleball came along. It was played on a handball court with rules similar to handball. The paddle was solid wood and heavy. The ball was somewhat like the inside of a tennis ball.

Iowa State had first-class athletic facilities. Beyer Hall, the student sports facility, was just across the street from my dorm and had several paddleball courts. The school also had excellent intramural leagues and highly competitive tournaments. During my college years there, from the fall of 1966 to the spring of 1970, I played competitive intramural paddleball with solid wooden paddles and then racquetball with clunky, wooden-framed, strung racquets. I won the Iowa State University paddleball tournament singles title my sophomore year and finished second in the tournament my junior year. In one of the paddleball tournaments, I played Ed Gagnier, the ISU gymnastics coach. (The Cyclones had a nationally ranked team.) Gagnier was good, and I recall he beat me. What I remember most is that he padded around the court wearing gymnastic "slippers" rather than tennis shoes. One paddleball match almost did me in. I was playing against Clyde Senters, an ISU football lineman who weighed in the lower three hundreds. During a rally, the leather wrist strap on his wooden paddle broke when he swung it. I was in front of him, and as I took a step, I slipped on some sweat on the court and fell slightly to my right. At the same moment, Senters's paddle flew by my head within inches of my left ear and crashed into the front wall. Had I not slipped, I might not be here today to share the memory.

When I moved to Rochester to begin work at IBM in 1970, I was pleased to see an outstanding group of racquetball players at the YMCA. I competed in the leagues and the tournaments (city, regional, and state) in Rochester and surrounding towns. Rochester's best (Mike Gorman, Fred Banfield, and Dick Carpenter) were out of my league when I began, but they were kind enough to let me play with them, and I gradually got better. I started to play my best racquetball around 1979. Here are some of my top finishes in the 1970s:

- 1st place in B singles at the Des Moines YMCA Open–1976
- 1st place in singles in the First Annual Joe's Liquor Tournament–1979
- 2nd place in the YMCA racquetball singles league–1978 and 1979
- 3rd place in the YMCA racquetball singles league–1973
- 3rd place in doubles in the Rochester City Tournament–1974 and 1979
- 3rd place in singles in the Rochester City Tournament–1975 and 1977
- Consolation singles champion at the Iowa State Open in Des Moines–1975

A word about the YMCA racquetball leagues: The Y had only two courts when I first started playing (until 1977, when four more were added). There were many players in league matches and just-for-fun matches vying for times. The two courts could be reserved but only a day (or two) in advance, by phone, starting at 9:00 AM. All who wanted a court would start dialing at 9:00 AM on the dot, hoping to get through before all slots were booked. Some IBM managers who played racquetball would have their secretaries call in their reservations for them. To fit more players in, our league matches were scheduled to start at 9:00 and 10:00 PM on weeknights. After a match, I wouldn't be home and asleep until 1:00 AM or later because I was so wound up. How did I do that and get up early for work?

Here's a note I made about one of my league matches:
Dave Winkle and I had our second league racquetball match, a really grueling affair that I won 21–18 and 21–15. I've been lucky this year (21 wins and 3 losses so far) to be able to win the close ones and not choke too badly. Good fun with a good friend!

1980s and 1990s

I continued to play competitive racquetball through the 1980s and early 1990s. The place to play in Rochester became the Supreme Court on Pennington Court north of, and across the highway from, IBM. Mike Gorman, the best player in the city (and one of the best in the state) managed the club. At the club's grand opening in 1979, I played an exhibition doubles match with Mike Miller against the Gorman/Ebbitt team.

Exhibition match at the Supreme Court's grand opening

The *Rochester Post Bulletin* published the photo above with the caption: It's Open! With a large crowd looking on, Jim Ebbitt, former city tennis pro, serves one up in a feature match on the glass court at the Supreme Court racquetball club as part of this weekend's grand opening celebration. Ebbitt's teammate at left is Supreme Court Pro Mike Gorman, and awaiting the serve are Mike Ransom (left) and Mike Miller. On the platform at right is Tom Wirkus, a pro from Rockford, Illinois, who refereed the match. Nearly 500 people turned out Friday for the opening. The tournament list below includes ones in which I did particularly well:

- 1st place in singles in the Second Annual Joe's Liquor Tournament–1980
- 1st place in singles in the Third Annual Joe's Liquor Tournament–1981
- 1st place in singles in the Mason City YMCA Tournament–1982
- 1st place in singles in the Rochester YMCA Member Tournament–1981
- 2nd place in singles (lost to Jim Ebbitt in finals) and 2nd place in doubles (Dave Trautmann and I lost to Gorman and Ebbitt) in the Rochester City Tournament–1980
- 2nd place in singles in the Mason City YMCA Tournament–1980
- 2nd place in doubles in the All Star Athletics Tournament–1980
- 2nd place in singles (lost to Dave Trautmann) and 2nd place in doubles (Dave Trautmann and I lost to Gorman and Ebbitt) in the Rochester City Tournament–1981

Here's a note I wrote after the 1980 Rochester City Tournament:
Racquetball, racquetball, racquetball. In singles I beat Dick Carpenter 21–7 and 21–7 in the semifinals. I then lost to Jim Ebbitt 21–20 and 21–16 in the finals. In the doubles finals, Dave Trautmann and I lost to Mike Gorman and Jim Ebbitt in three games, winning the first 21–20, losing the second 21–7, and losing the tiebreaker 11–9. A great match.

Leg cramps, stomach muscle cramps, and exhaustion. If it weren't in my blood, I'd have given up the game long ago, but it's something I enjoy, the competition and feeling of playing well. Losing doesn't bother me as long as I give 100% and play well. And if I can help others see how they can play for fun and exercise, I'm happy. Someday, when my legs, arms, and shoulders go, I'll have to find another sport.

In the 1980 City Racquetball Tournament, I lost to Jim Ebbitt in the Championship game.

    I dominated the IBM Watson Trophy Racquetball Annual Tournament. It began in 1981 owing to the immense popularity of the sport among IBMers. Hundreds of players and their spouses competed in multiple brackets. In nine years of tournament singles competition, I lost only one match. I won the top-bracket singles title in the years from 1981 to 1985, 1988 to 1989, and in 1991. My partner and I won the doubles title in 1987 and 1991.

    In 1981 I finished first in the top bracket. In my last two matches, I beat John McConnell 21–16 and 21–7 and Dave Winkle 21–20, 11–21, and 11–6. My legs were tired and I didn't play my best, but I still won. I was sick and missed the tournament in 1986. The following year I played only doubles because I was tired and stressed from moving into our new home and being super busy at work. My doctor prescribed two days' rest at home not long before the tournament. Dave Winkle and I won the doubles title. In 1989, I didn't lose a game in three singles matches. I beat Pat Revlin 3–0, Scott Oeltjen 3–0, and Dave Winkle 3–0 in the finals. In 1990, I lost in singles for the first time. George Selke beat me in the finals. In the semifinals, I played Bruce Johnson and lost the first two games of five but won the last three. It was a tough match with lots of long rallies and diving. In 1991,

I won the singles and doubles titles. In singles, I beat Bill Yonker and Curt Mathiowetz, and in doubles, with Steve Bluhm, beat the previous year's B-doubles winners.

A note about IBM-sponsored sports and Watson trophies. IBM provided year-round team and individual sports leagues and tournaments for their employees and spouses in basketball, bowling, golf, touch football, pistol shooting, racquetball, slow-pitch softball, trap shooting, tennis, and volleyball. The Watson Trophy dinner was held annually in the company's cafeteria, where trophies were awarded to the winners, and nationally known sports figures spoke. The event was named in honor of T. J. Watson, IBM CEO from 1914 to 1956. From 1971 to 1991 I had the good fortune of attending seventeen dinners through winning touch football, slow-pitch softball, volleyball, and racquetball titles. Speakers included Fran Tarkenton, Ray Nitschke, Rod Carew, Tom Gorman (MLB umpire), Ralph Kiner, George Plimpton, Jerry Kramer, Art Holst (NFL referee), Rosy Grier, Rocky Bleier, Janet Guthrie, Dave Winfield, John Wooden, Jim Ryan (track star), Steve Garvey, and Bruce Jenner. Spouses were invited to the dinner, too. One year that I didn't win a trophy, Jeanine did (in volleyball), so I was able to attend as her guest.

Most Meaningful Tournament
At the end of October 1980, I played in the Mason City YMCA tournament. I beat Bob Johnson (from Mason City) on Friday night and Jim Shields (from Elgin, Illinois) and Don Cameron (from Rochester) on Saturday. On Sunday, I lost in the championship game to Randy Snook, the Mason City club pro, 19–21 and 14–21. I had him in the first game 16–6 but couldn't hold on. I felt strong and played well all weekend. The most gratifying part of the tournament was that Dad got a chance to see all my games and see me play well. You could tell how proud he was to be my dad, and he overheard complimentary things about my attitude and sportsmanship that made him even prouder. For me, allowing him to enjoy those times was more important than winning. The next year I returned to Mason City to play again in its tournament. I won, beating Dave Flor from Albert Lea in the championship match.

After tough racquetball matches, I would be dripping with sweat, as was the case here in my loss to Randy Snook in the finals.

Most Interesting Request
A long-time friend Jerry (not his real name) asked an interesting favor of me regarding his brother-in-law, who lived in the Twin Cities. Miles (also not his real name) was a lawyer, a Porsche club member, and the kind of guy who liked to drape his sweater around his neck. Jerry thought Miles was a bit too "caught up" in himself. Miles played racquetball at a club in the Cities and told Jerry he played a pretty good game. Jerry asked if I would be willing to get a court at the Y for a match with Miles, whom I had not met. Then he added this unusual request: "I would like it if you didn't let him score a point." So I didn't, and Jerry still talks about the match to this day. After it was over Miles told Jerry, "I knew I was in trouble when, getting suited up in the locker room, I saw Mike's washboard abs. He was in some kind of shape!"

Toughest Loss
From 1978 to 1982 I played a lot of racquetball with Dave Trautmann, one of the best young racquetball players to come out of Rochester (along with Ed Graddy, Dave Graddy, and Bill Crowson). Dave's dad, Jim, asked me if I would help his son learn the game, and I did, beginning when Dave was in eighth or ninth grade. We spent many hours at the Supreme Court and at the Y. Dave had outstanding abilities and a focus and intensity that were unreal. I remember clearly the first practice game he won—I never let him beat me; he had to earn it. He took off from there and never looked back.

THE OLDER I GET THE BETTER I WAS

Racquetball doubles with Dave Trautmann

Dave and I played many a tournament doubles game together, beating some pretty good players along the way. In one tournament at the Supreme Court, we beat Jim and Joe Wirkus, at the time two of the best racquetball players in Wisconsin. In early March 1980, Dave and I won the open doubles bracket of the Rochester Heart Fund Racquetball Tournament. In the semifinals, we beat Mark Ramlo and Jerry Ewelling, an excellent team from Austin, 11–10 in the tie breaker. In the finals, we beat Dave Warner and Arnold Chastine 21–10 and 21–20. In March 1981, I played Dave in the Rochester City Championship. I beat him in the first game and was ahead of him in the second, but he turned it on, came from behind to beat me, and then skunked me 11–0 in the third. I ran out of gas, and his seventeen years–younger legs and arm were too strong for me. If I had to lose, I'm glad that Dave was the one who beat me. The title match with Dave plus all the matches—singles and doubles—I played leading up to it, took a toll on me. I was sick in bed for almost a week after the tournament.

Jeanine remembers watching me and Dave warming up for a doubles match in Winona. A woman looked down at us from the viewing area and said, "Oh, who are those boys down there?" Jeanine said, "Well, one of those boys is Dave Trautmann, who is seventeen, and the other one is my thirty-four-year-old husband!"

Racquetball Hall of Fame
The Rochester Racquetball Hall of Fame was formed in 1989 to honor the top players, as well as those who supported the game. In 1996 I was the eighth person elected; the previous inductees were:
 1989: Fred Banfield
 1990: Mike Gorman
 1991: Chuck Hazama
 1992: Dee Lichty
 1993: Dick Carpenter
 1994: John Brandrup
 1995: Sheryl Warfield

I was honored to be elected to the Rochester Racquetball of Hall of Fame. Left to right: Mike Gorman, Fred Banfield, Sheryl Warfield, me, Dee Lichty, and Dick Carpenter.

THE OLDER I GET THE BETTER I WAS

When I came to Rochester in the 1970s, the best racquetball players my age or slightly older were Mike Gorman, Dick Carpenter, and Fred Banfield. I was extremely honored to join them in the Hall of Fame. Dad, Mom, Ben, Jeanine, and her mom were among the sixty or seventy people in attendance at the Rochester Athletic Club the evening of my induction. Mike Gorman introduced me. The text of my talk follows:

> I am truly honored to be a member of the Racquetball Hall of Fame, and I appreciate all of the nice comments that have been made tonight. I'm 47, and at that point in my life where I agree with what the golfer Chi Chi Rodriquez says: The older I get the better I was!
>
> Mike [Gorman] hit some of the highlights of my career, but it would be only fair to mention a lowlight, too. I think it was in the mid-1970s I played in the State Tournament, which was then held in Rochester. I had the misfortune of playing Steve Strandemo[1] in the first or second round. He would soon turn professional. To say I was nervous would be an understatement, and I'm not sure if I scored a point in the two games. Not only did Strandemo keep his warm-up suit on for both games, but I joke that he didn't take the head cover off his racquet either.
>
> Mike said it would be ok to take a few minutes tonight to reminisce about the past and what racquetball has meant to me, so I'll try to be brief, but I do have some things I'd like to share.
>
> First of all, I'd like to introduce my family who are here:
>
> My wife, Jeanine, who deserves tremendous thanks for all the hours she's spent in YMCA athletic clubs and gymnasiums cheering for me as I competed not only in racquetball, but also in volleyball, softball, running, and tennis.
>
> My son, Ben, my folks, Jim and Barbara, and my mother-in-law, Jean Brose. And a special thanks to Dave Trautmann, a great

---

[1] *Strandemo grew up in Kenyon, Minnesota, and would become one of the first in the state to turn professional. He maintained a top-ten national ranking from 1973 to 1986, and in 2005 he was inducted into the USA Racquetball Hall of Fame.*

friend and probably the best young racquetball player to come out of Rochester, who drove here from Shoreview, Minnesota, just to be part of the evening. When I look back on the thirty years I've been playing racquetball, my thoughts fall into four areas: the game itself, the personal test the game provides, the people, and sportsmanship.

The Game: The game of racquetball is basically the same now as when I began playing it. Oh, the equipment and players have gotten much better, but the game is still like a sweaty chess match in a room. You're trying to think two shots ahead to set up a shot. You're jockeying for position. As most of you know, there's no better feeling than getting hot in a match and rolling out backhands and forehands, diving for balls and seeing them roll out for winners as you're sprawled on the floor, or coming back from being down 10–5 in a final game to win 11–10.

And it's a game where being close to the floor is an advantage. So, it's kind of nice to be only 5 feet 8 inches. It's been fun to beat some pretty big guys who would just as soon hit the ball through you as around you if they had the chance. I love playing the game now as much as I did thirty years ago.

The Test: Racquetball provides a test of what you're made of. I've had matches where I was sure I was going to lose my lunch on the court, or where I wasn't sure I'd be able to take another breath. But then you look over at your opponent and see he might not be in any better shape than you, so you dig down deep and get to find out what's there. It's like the marathon runner who glides through the first twenty miles, then hits the wall, and the last six miles are like running through hell. I've competed in lots of sports, but racquetball is I think the toughest, but because of that it has been the most rewarding.

The People: There are so many fine people I've met through racquetball. I wish I had the time to talk about them all. Mike Gorman is simply the best. He deserves to sit at the head of the table in the Racquetball Hall of Fame. We've been friends since the early 1970s and have played so many games over the years. He's beaten me in every match that counted except one that happened years ago in a City Tournament. I think he could give me

THE OLDER I GET THE BETTER I WAS

a 14–0 lead right now and walk out on the court and beat me 15–14 if he really wanted to. And then he'd say it was just luck.

Since I've gotten away from playing in the open brackets, I'll see Mike and ask him, "Who's the best player in town these days?" He always gives me that smile and says, "We are, aren't we?" We still play for fun, and we are starting to bet on whose back is going to go out first each year.

Fred Banfield: I wish each of you here tonight had the pleasure of watching Fred Banfield play. I've never played against anyone with more intensity. Fred was always screaming at himself, his racquet, the ball, or me. And after the match I could count on Fred to give me an accurate assessment. He'd look me in the eye and say, "You played like crap and deserved to lose," or he'd tell me that he played great or that I played great and deserved to win. In any case, he'd play fair and square during our matches and we would shake hands as friends after.

Dave Trautmann: Mike has already told you a bit about how much I think of Dave Trautmann. Dave's thirty-two now, and we were talking today about how much fun we had when we both were much younger. I am so proud to have been able to help him learn the game, not just the shots and the strategy, but also how to go about being a good sport, too.

I could go on and on with stories about how much I've enjoyed playing with Scott Litin, Dave Winkle, all the Graddys, the younger Gormans, Carp, John Brandrup, Dee Lichty, Bill Crowson, Guy Paradise, and more, but I'm sure I'd leave someone out, and I would hate to do that. Let's just say it's been a blast, and I really appreciate all the good times I've had with everyone.

Sportsmanship: Many of us in this room have collected plenty of trophies and honors. When I look back, the two trophies I'm most proud of are the one for winning the Mason City Open Singles, and that's because my dad was there to see me play and win, and the 1976 Sportsman of the Year Award I received from the YMCA, because I have always put being a good sport on a par with winning.

I think our real trophies in life are our friends and family members who help us enjoy the good times like these and who will also stick by us in the not-so-good times. I've always considered myself lucky to have such a good family and so many friends.

So, tonight I say thanks to the Hall of Fame Committee for presenting me with this honor. It means a lot to me. I will do my best to uphold the tradition and standards you've set. I say congratulations to the winners and participants in the city tournament and thanks to the RAC and its racquetball committee for making this night possible.

Finally, thanks for taking time to listen to an old racquetball player share how much the game has meant to him, and I encourage you all to keep on playing and promoting the sport!

I commend Mike Gorman for initiating the Hall of Fame and leading it for many years. He handed the Hall's leadership to Rick Schact, one of the best Rochester players to follow Mike. Rick was voted into the Minnesota State Racquetball Hall of Fame in 2013.

John Rice

On a Monday evening in March 1998, I got a call from John Rice, an "older" fellow who had been inducted into the Racquetball Hall of Fame earlier that month. I had not been able to attend the induction party, but I had taken a few minutes to write the brief letter (below) that I mailed to him:

Dear John, Congratulations on joining the Rochester Racquetball Hall of Fame! I am sorry I can't be at your induction in person, but I wanted to say, "Nice going" in writing. I was very honored to join the likes of Mike Gorman, John Brandrup, Sheryl Warfield, and several others when I joined the Hall of Fame, and I hope you feel the same. You've been an avid and excellent racquetball player for so many years. I will always remember you as a perfect gentleman on and off the court, which is what all sports need more of these days. Racquetball is a wonderful game. It keeps us young and in shape, humbled at times, and along the way helps us encounter wonderful people such as you. Take care.

John had called to thank me and tell me that the letter was "the nicest one he had ever received." Here's a man, now in his upper sixties I imagine, who just received the nicest letter in his life from me! It took me but a few minutes to write it, but what I wrote was from the heart, and it obviously had a big impact. John's words made me feel incredibly good, to have been able to make him feel that pleased with his accomplishment. It was a moment that reminded me of what life is all about—using your time and talents to be kind to others.

The Best
During my racquetball prime, Mike Gorman was the premier player in Rochester, our Mr. Racquetball. I wrote an article about him that was published in the September 2005 issue of the *Generations of Today* magazine. Here's an excerpt:

> Though Mike dislikes talking about any of his tournament victories ("I don't keep track of such things," he says), he won a multitude of singles and doubles city championships, state championships in his age bracket, and even a third place in a national tournament. Anyone who played racquetball in Rochester in the seventies and eighties knew that Mike was the force in town. Dick Carpenter (another excellent racquetball player) recalls how local players emulated Mike. "If Mike bought a certain brand of racquet, soon there would be a run on that racquet at the local sporting goods stores. If he wore a certain shirt, players would be wearing the same the next week. We kidded Mike about this. His only response would be to give us that sly smile of his. Mike was the quiet leader with the big heart that we all looked up to."

When Mike's racquetball game was at its best, he began to experience (and had to overcome) several obstacles off the court, which I recounted in the *Today* article. His midlife corrections were even more impressive than his sports accomplishments. Fellow racquetball player Scott Litin kidded me and Mike about the article. He said, "If Ransom can make Gorman look like such a saint, I can't wait for him to write an article about me!"

I Will Always Remember…
I was asked to give a brief talk and introduce Ed Graddy into the Rochester Racquetball Hall of Fame in April 2000. Ed, his brother Dave, and Dave Trautmann were three from Rochester who started at a young age and became outstanding players. I visited with Ed to get some material for my talk. During our conversation, I asked him, "Do you remember the first time you first beat your dad on the racquetball court?" (Jim Graddy was an excellent player and also a member of the

Hall of Fame.) Ed looked at me, smiled, and said, "No, I don't, but I remember the first time I beat you." It reminded me of the saying, "You never know when you're making a memory." Looking back on my racquetball years, more than the wins and trophies, I feel I set a good example for the younger players by playing hard and valuing good sportsmanship as much (or more) than I did winning.

Squash

I won't give it up until I'm old.

With Lindsey and Ben. Ben and I had just won the C doubles bracket of the St. Paul Commodore Squash Club's tournament, circa 2013.

Of all the sports I've played, squash is the one I've taken up most recently. The Rochester Athletic Club (RAC) has two squash courts that I used to walk by on my way to their multiple racquetball courts. My interest in racquetball waned around 2001. I'm not sure why; I'd been an "addicted" player for about thirty years. It provided excellent exercise, but maybe I lost enthusiasm because I could no longer compete at the highest levels. My friend Bob Waite, with whom I worked at IBM and ran frequently, had played squash in his younger years. In 2003, Bob came along with me a few times as my guest, we booked a squash court, and he introduced me to playing the game. I caught on fairly quickly and soon was competing with other squash players at the club. Ben began playing the game, too, and he joined the Commodore Squash Club near his and Lindsey's condo in St. Paul. I joined the club, too, and he and I played there whenever we could. The Commodore had one doubles squash court. Ben and I entered a Commodore squash tournament and won the C doubles bracket. It was much fun. The next year, we moved up to the B doubles bracket and didn't do so well, but we gave it our best shot.

Speaking of the Commodore Squash Club reminds me of the time my cousin Randy Forzano, his wife, Robin, and their daughters Jenna and Julieanne were visiting for a few days in 2014. While Jeanine, Robin, and the girls shopped at Mall of America, I thought it would be a good time for me to introduce Randy to the game of squash at the Club. Randy is ten years younger than me. We have had more of a brotherly than "cousinly" relationship, the seeds of which were planted back in the 1960s during one of my family's visits with his in East Liverpool, Ohio, and then nurtured with nearly annual visits back and forth between our hometowns. Talk about a good sport; Randy is up for any athletic adventure I might suggest (like biking across Iowa, which I will detail in a later chapter). Randy and I have an hour workout on the squash court. He likes the game, and we're a "good tired" after. We have some time to kill, so I say, "Randy, since you don't get to St. Paul often, what would you think of walking over to the University of St. Thomas to check out their campus?" Ben had gone to college there, the walk along Summit Avenue is a scenic one, and it would be fun to show Randy around. I wasn't as "in tune' with

THE OLDER I GET THE BETTER I WAS

St. Paul then as I am now; I thought St. Thomas was a mile or two away.

"Sure thing," said Randy, typical of his enthusiasm. So off we march on a hot summer afternoon for a "short walk." Much to my surprise, the St. Thomas campus is *six* miles from the squash club, not a mile or two. As we trudge along, I keep thinking we are getting close, but that is not to be. Fortunately, we come upon some young girls who have set up a lemonade stand on the way that helps us quench our thirst. The trip back is grueling. Jeanine, Robin, and the girls are waiting for us to pick them up and wondering where we are. Randy and I have walked *twelve* miles after a tiring squash workout. He has never let me forget that misadventure, and I don't blame him for reminding me.

Squash provides an incredibly intense workout. Rallies are much longer than in racquetball because the squash ball is much less lively, and you have to avoid hitting a 17-inch tin strip that runs along the bottom of the court's front wall. When the ball hits the tin, you lose the point or your serve. In racquetball, one wants to "kill" the ball and end a rally in as few shots as possible. In squash, the strategy is to keep the ball in play until your opponent makes a mistake rather than you make a winning shot. I'm not as patient as I should be; I go for the kill too often. I've lost to players who are not as fit or athletic as I am but who are much better at placing shots and waiting for me to make a mistake.

My most regular partner in squash was Guy Paradise. We played a lot of racquetball together over the years, too, before we transitioned to squash, and I enjoyed every match. He's fifteen years younger and a fine friend. I kept pace with him for many years, but he gradually began to the get the best of me as I aged from sixty to seventy. I don't have regular squash partners at the Commodore in St. Paul, but through their "all comers" nights and tournaments I've met several with whom I've enjoyed playing. Singles squash is as physically demanding a sport as any I've played. I wish I could have begun the game in the 1970s and '80s when I was in my best court shape. I hesitate to give it up, because doing so will be another concession that I've grown old.

Golf
Not one but two Masters Tournaments

With Ben at the 2019 Masters Golf Tournament. We are standing by the 160-year-old oak in front of the Augusta National clubhouse.

Growing up, golf—to me—was a game played by people with money, which my family didn't have. That's what made our vacations with my Forzano aunt, uncle, and cousins in East Liverpool, Ohio, so exciting: They were members of a country club a short walk from their home. The club had a golf course, swimming pool, tennis courts, dining area, and nine-hole putting green. Though Clear Lake had a nice "vacation" nine-hole golf course, the Veterans Memorial Golf Course, my first golfing experiences took place at the East Liverpool Country Club. I wasn't a natural. I batted left handed but golfed right handed because left-handed clubs were hard to find. I bought my first set of clubs (right handed) from Dad's friend Harry Bovaird. I think I paid him twenty-five dollars for the bag (tartan plaid) and clubs. The set looked like something you'd buy with Gold Bond Stamps. I was probably in high school. I don't recall golfing much at all, but in the summer of 1969, between my junior and senior years in college, when I stayed in Ames and worked at the Iowa State University computer center, I golfed with some coworkers on my twenty-first birthday at a course near Nevada, east of Ames.

I rarely golfed in my early years at IBM. I didn't think it was a sport because one didn't exercise hard enough to need a shower after a round. To get a real workout, I thought one should go for a long run first and then play golf, or that golf should be a combination of elapsed time and score. Also, for my outdoor sporting activities in the 1960s and 1970s, I disliked wearing a shirt. Ben has kidded me about why I was shirtless in so many of my photos from those decades. "Didn't you own shirts back then?" he's asked. The Soldiers Field course in Rochester has a "Shoes and Shirts Required" sign. I remember the day I saw that and couldn't figure out why one should have to wear a shirt. Shoes I could understand, but not the shirt.

In the mid-to-late 1980s, I became hooked on golf (and golf shirts). I started playing multiple times a week with Jim Gilkinson, Dave Winkle, and Fred Huss. (Also, I played plenty of tennis with them.) John Noseworthy and family moved to Rochester around 1990. John, Jim, and I golfed many rounds at Soldiers Field, oftentimes playing just the front or back nine. I switched to golfing left handed, took lessons, watched videos, and read many instruction books. I may have improved over the years at golf more than I improved in any other sport because of my commitment to practice and determination to be a decent golfer. I envied the "natural" golfers, those you could tell had learned golf and competed in the sport at an early age. Their swings were smooth and fluid, their short games were impressive, and they played their best under pressure.

Though I broke forty many times for nine holes, I believe I broke eighty for eighteen holes only once or twice. I never kept an official handicap; I was probably a twelve or a fourteen in my prime.

The Freeze Your Golf Ball (FYGB) Tournament

I golfed many rounds with Rod Morlock. On October 8, 1991, he sent me the following email that planted the seed for what would become an annual golf tournament on the first Friday of every October, mainly for IBM golfers; it would continue for twenty years and attract up to a hundred guys for each event.

> How about me delegating something to you…sending out an inquiry on the first annual ransom/morlock fygb tourney. Friday aft oct 18 at 1:30 at one of golf courses in town. Best shot…either three or four person teams depending on number of entrants. $5 entry/person, teams will be formed based on handicap actual/estimated. rhm/mjr final arbitrators on handicaps. Feel better if you sent out Mike…what day do you think… I think it's MEA weekend so not sure if that will affect tee times or # of entrants. People I would send it to: Hedger, Larson, Mike Garry, Sandstrom, Harens, Dick Valde, Les Stolte, Dave Dutelle, Gene Leitner. You should add your names. If these guys want to recruit some others, great. Perhaps if we get 12 names, we could have 4 3-person team. give me a call.

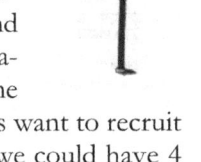

We had enough responses to proceed with the tournament on October 18 and things were all set up at Soldiers Field, but it (fittingly) snowed a half an inch the morning of the tournament, the course closed, and FYGB was off to an inauspicious start. The next year, we decided to play the course in Adams on the first Friday in October (the date it would remain from then on). Dozens of golfers enjoyed a sunny, eighty-two-degree day, and FYGB was off and running.

Rod and I became known for hosting an organized, well-run, no-frills, lots-of-fun tournament. We put in much work during the weeks leading up to it to ensure it went smoothly. We advertised the event as one that would be played rain, shine, sleet, or snow—as long as the course was open, the tournament would go on. The format was a four-person team scramble. Teams were flighted to try to give each a fair chance. Prize money was given for first, second, and third finishers in each flight plus holes were selected for long drive, closest to the pin, long putt, etc. A meal (burgers, brats, beans, potato salad…) was served after the event, prize money was awarded, and then we departed. Rod, though an IBM executive, is a farmer at heart. To add a "farming touch" to the tournament, we required teams to tee off on the first hole wearing Fleet Farm yellow farm gloves. The guys had a blast with that.

As you can see from the tournament history that follows, we had a wide range of weather conditions, from a high of eighty-two degrees to a low in the thirties, from bright sun to sleet and snow, from calm to gale-force winds. As the years went by, it seemed that the players had the most fun during the most miserable weather. Talk to any veteran FYGB players and they'll likely recall a story from Hidden Creek in 1999 or Wabasha in 2004. It became a badge of honor to tough out the bad-weather FYGBs.

1991: Soldiers Field (one-half inch of snow; no tournament due to course being closed)
1992: Adams (82 degrees, sunny)
1993: Maple Valley (40s, cloudy, windy)
1994: Chatfield (40s, cloudy, windy)
1995: Lake City Golf Club (low 50s, drizzle)
1996: Willow Creek (cloudy, 50s)
1997: Hidden Creek, Owatonna (70s/80s, sunny)
1998: Willow Creek (50s/60s, partly cloudy)
1999: Hidden Creek (low 30s; sleet/snow; an inch of snow on some parts of course); our most miserable FYGB)
2000: Meadow Lakes (cold, cloudy; some snow flurries; mid 40s)
2001: Mt. Frontenac (cold, dry; high 40s, windy)

THE OLDER I GET THE BETTER I WAS

2002: Mt. Frontenac (lousy day; low 50s and temps dropping; raining when we started; 30+ mph winds; intermittent rain, drizzle, dry; sun peeked out a couple of times)
2003: Lake City Golf Club (low 50s, cool, cloudy)
2004: Wabasha (40s, windy, freezing rain most of day; second most miserable FYGB)
2005: Zumbrota (low 60s; super golf day)
2006: Zumbrota (sunny, breezy, 60s)
2007: Dodge Center (mid 60s, partly cloudy, two-club wind)
2008: Eastwood Golf Course (mid 70s, sunny, and calm)
2009: The Oaks, Hayfield (40 to 50 degrees and rain/drizzle the whole time, but no wind; Mark Kalmes has a hole in one!)
2010: The Jewel, Lake City (beautiful day, 70s)

Since our last tournament ten years ago, on the first Friday of every October I take note of the weather and think of the fun our FYGB golfers would be having in it whether good or bad.

Turtle Creek

One of my most memorable golf outings occurred in Florida in the late 1980s. Jeanine, Ben, Jeanine's mom, my dad, and I were going on a baseball spring training vacation in Orlando. (At that time, the Minnesota Twins trained there at Tinker Field.) My uncle Ross had planned to come, but at the last minute he couldn't. We asked Jim Gilkinson to fill in for him, and he said yes. Jim loves baseball, golf, and tennis. At the Indoor Tennis Club, a few weeks before we left, Jim and I visited with Larry Osterwise, the IBM Plant General Manager, after a tennis match. When we mentioned our trip to Florida, he said we should check out a golf course he had heard was a really good one called Turtle Creek, a course not far from Orlando. Larry either vacationed near there or somehow knew about it.

Turtle Creek was a top-notch, semiprivate course. Jim and I golfed mainly public courses. Fancy courses tended to psych us out and put a little extra pressure on our game. If we were invited to golf at the Rochester Country Club, for example, it was a big deal. I called Turtle Creek and made a reservation for us to play. I told Jim that the person I talked to seemed obsessed about noting that golfers must wear collared shirts. He mentioned it multiple times during our phone call. I noted the importance of this to Jim several times, too, to make sure he'd pack his collared shirt. I worried that if any of us forgot to wear one, we'd end up in a Florida prison. They also noted that Dad would have to pay a fee just to ride along with us in the golf cart. Just another sign of how exclusive this place was. One concession to the high-priced golf was that the pro mentioned the green fees included a free lunch for us all, even for Dad.

Frank Earnest, a friend who had moved from Rochester and lived an hour or so drive from the course, joined us. He, Jim, Dad, and I arrived, enthused and excited, all wearing our collared shirts on a beautiful Florida March spring day. (Dad wore a collared shirt, too, even though he was just riding.) It would be an understatement to say that we were pumped, nervous, and ready to begin our round.

Things took a turn immediately after we drove into the parking lot. As we were getting our clubs out of the trunk, a perky clubhouse assistant pulled up in a snazzy golf cart, ready to load our golf bags onto it for our round. Jim and I looked at each other. Yikes! We weren't used to this kind of treatment. Could we decline his offer? Did we tip the guy? In hindsight, it seems like our golf wheels started to fall off as we watched him strap our clubs to our cart.

We had allowed ourselves plenty of time to hit balls before we teed off. We checked in and headed to the range, one like none we had seen before. It was a giant lake *into* which (not *over* which) you hit your range balls. This seemed appropriate when we looked at the course layout; there was water on fourteen of the eighteen holes. You had to carry water on six of the holes. Osterwise had not mentioned this. With each ball we blasted into the giant lake, Jim and I grew more worried about what awaited us on the course.

And what a disaster it was. Jim and Frank could break eighty on a good day; I usually shot in the mid to upper eighties. That day, I'm not sure if any of us broke one hundred. We shanked, lofted, hooked, sliced, and sclaffed balls into every body of water on the course. Frank ran out of balls before the back nine. None of us had ever been part of such a fiasco.

When we weren't in the water, we were in the sand. After about eight holes, Jim and I started complaining that it was odd that such a pricey course with so much sand wouldn't have rakes by the bunkers. In the midst of one of those whinings, Jim noticed that every cart, ours included, had a rake on it for our personal use. Just another thing to psych us out.

We finished our eighteen holes and staggered into the clubhouse, thinking that even though we had golfed miserably, we'd at least get a free lunch out of the deal. We, and not the course, would have the last laugh. At the restaurant, when we mentioned this, our waiter informed us that the offer was only good on Tuesdays, and it wasn't a Tuesday. So, in the end, Turtle Creek did get the last laugh.

On the ride home, Dad totaled up the damage. "Jim," he said, "looks like you shot a 115." Jim didn't say a word; just accepted it as his punishment. "Oh, wait," Dad said a few minutes later. "I made a mistake; you had a 105, not 115." Jim had to laugh about having such a bad round that he didn't even notice an added ten strokes.

After coming home, at our next Saturday tennis session at the club, we told Osterwise that we had golfed Turtle Creek. "Really," he said. "I'd like to hear what you thought about it. I've never golfed there; it's much too expensive for me!"

From that day forward, if Jim or I were ever having a bad day on the golf course, we would look at each other and say, "Well, at least it's not as bad as Turtle Creek!"

The 2016 Masters
The Masters. To anyone who loves golf, upon hearing these two words, their eyes mist over, and they hear angels strumming harps in the background. The Masters Golf Tournament, held each year since 1934 at the Augusta National Golf Club in Augusta, Georgia, is one of the toughest tickets to score in all of sports. Think World Series, Super Bowl, Final Four, Cooperstown, Kentucky Derby, and Fenway Park all rolled into one. Walking the course is like walking through paradise. (Don Sutton, Baseball Hall of Famer once said, "If you don't get goose bumps when you come into this place, you don't have a pulse.")

Augusta is renowned for its impeccable grounds. Pine straw is imported, bird chirps and tweets are played on inconspicuous speakers, and even the ponds were once dyed blue. The club is famed for its azaleas and dogwoods. Spectators, called "patrons," are reverential, hushed, and tread lightly on the hallowed ground. If you break into a run, an Augusta marshal will remind you that running is not allowed. Don't even think of littering. For all other PGA tournaments, marshals hold up QUIET signs when a golfer addresses a ball. No one holds up signs at the Masters. The patrons *know* they must behave.

PGA golfers think the Masters is special, too. Dave Marr said, "At my first Masters, I got the feeling that if I didn't play well, I wouldn't go to heaven." Bobby Jones, the club cofounder, said, "I shall never forget my first visit to the property which is now Augusta National. The long lane of magnolias through which we approached was beautiful. The old manor house was charming. The rare trees and shrubs of the nursery were enchanting. But when I walked out on the grass terrace under the big trees behind the house and looked down over the property, the experience was unforgettable. It seemed the land had been lying there for years just waiting for someone to lay a golf course upon it."

All electronic devices, including cameras and cell phones, are forbidden, so patrons are isolated from friends, families, work, and the rest of the world's busyness and can only focus on the golfing drama that unfolds before them. Though people pay an arm and a leg for tickets, once inside the grounds, the concession prices are extremely reasonable. The classic pimento cheese sandwiches are a $1.50 each, domestic beer is $4 a cup, and imported beer is only a dollar more. Though the lines in the merchandise areas are long, the prices are reasonable there, too.

Growing up, I was so involved with baseball, volleyball, tennis, and racquetball that I did not pay much attention to golf. Any sport, I thought, where you don't play hard enough to work up a sweat, isn't really a sport. In the late 1980s, though, I became addicted to the game. I started taking lessons, watching instructional videos, and playing multiple times a week. I envied the natural golfers, those you could tell had learned golf and competed in the sport at an early age. They had fluid swings, flawless short games, and carded their best scores under

THE OLDER I GET THE BETTER I WAS

pressure. As my love for golf grew, I became fascinated with the Masters. Practice round tickets (Monday through Wednesday) were available to the public, but tickets to Thursday through Sunday for the tournament action were impossible to get. I thought I had a better chance of walking on the moon than ever attending a Masters Tournament in person. But one must learn never to think never.

In December 2015, an opportunity arose to obtain two tickets to the Masters. Not only I, but also my wife (Jeanine), son (Ben), daughter-in-law (Lindsey), and granddaughter (Greta, eleven months) would be going. Ben and I pored over the course layout before we went and decided on the best places to view the action. One perk that I found hard to believe is that if you have an official Masters folding chair (which we were able to obtain), you can set it up to reserve your spot. Hundreds if not thousands of spectators arrive well before the gates open and stand in line to rush in and place their chairs in prime spots, either around the eighteenth green or wherever else they might want to be. They can roam about the course knowing they can return at any time to where they've left their chairs. Another perk is that more than one person can share the same ticket. This meant that with two tickets, Ben, Lindsey, Jeanine, and I could each spend time at the tournament.

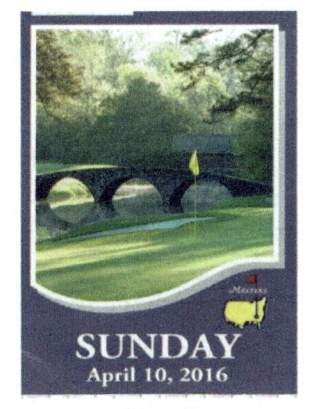

Ben found lodging for us in Aiken, South Carolina, about twenty miles from Augusta. Aiken is a town of about 31,000 in horse country. We flew into Atlanta on Friday, April 8, and drove up past Augusta to Aiken to stay our first night there. The excitement of a Saturday and Sunday at the Masters is like none other. Waking that Saturday morning, I couldn't believe that we were soon to experience it. Our plan was for Ben and me to attend Saturday while Jeanine and Lindsey, with Greta, shopped and dined in Aiken. I'll long remember us walking the hallowed Masters grounds our very first time. I'd seen the course and its beauty on TV, but there's no comparison to being there in person, to be part of the crowd milling around, to hear the roars in the distance when a golfer makes an unbelievable shot, to see the numbers on the old-school leaderboard (think the baseball scoreboard at Fenway Park), and to hear the crowd's murmurs when the leaderboard changes.

On Saturday, Ben and I watched Bubba Watson tee off on the first hole with his pink-shafted driver, and then we worked our way to the tee box (at the top of a hill) for No. 6 (a par 3) to see four twosomes play through. One of the golfers was Larry Mize, a senior golfer who had won the Masters in 1987. (Past winners are invited to play each year.) It was breezy, and I remember the golfers having a tough time reading the wind, which was much stronger above the trees than down below. It was a neat hole at which to begin. We were behind the golfers when they teed off, so we could see the ball soar high in the air before plopping down on the green far below. Then we spent most of the afternoon on the fifteenth fairway (a par 5), where we could watch the golfers' approach shots to the green. On Sunday, Jeanine and Lindsey spent the morning at the tournament, and then Ben and I got to spend Sunday afternoon at the Masters. We watched Brooks Koepka and Bryson DeChambeau (then an amateur) tee off on the first hole. Then we followed Sergio Garcia and Bubba Watson on Nos. 10, 11, and 12 before moving to what became our favorite location, beside and behind No. 7 (a par 4) green. The first twosome at No. 7 was Matthew Fitzpatrick and Jamie Donaldson, and thirteen more would follow, the last pair being Jordan Spieth and Smylie Kaufman. After watching them, we headed to the eighteenth green to watch golfers finish their rounds. We had to stand, but we were hole high, up a bit on the side of a hill, and just a few yards off the green.

Jordan Spieth was the favorite to win the tournament. He had won in 2015, his first major win, when he shot a 270 (18 under par) and pocketed $1.8 million. He tied the seventy-two-hole record set by Tiger Woods in 1997 and became the second youngest golfer (behind Woods) to win the Masters. He then won the 2015 U.S. Open with a score of 5 under par. He was the youngest U.S. Open champion since amateur Bobby Jones in 1923. He followed up with a win in the 2015 Tour Championship, which clinched the 2015 FedEx Cup for him.

Spieth led from the first round and built a five-shot lead going to the back nine on Sunday, but he lost six shots to par over the next three holes (not too long after we had seen him at No. 7), culminating in a quadruple-bogey on the twelfth hole, where he hit two balls into

THE OLDER I GET THE BETTER I WAS

Rae's Creek. Ben and I were standing near the eighteenth green beneath a TV broadcast booth and could hear announcers tell of Spieth's meltdown at the twelfth. The crowd gasped when the scoreboard showed Spieth's score on the hole. Danny Willett shot a bogey-free 67 (and an overall 5 under par) to win his first major championship, three strokes ahead of runners-up Lee Westwood and Spieth, who suffered one of the biggest collapses in Masters history.

The 2019 Masters
We thought that it would be hard to top our 2016 Masters experience, but 2019 was even better. Another opportunity arose for us to obtain two tickets for the full week, which included practice rounds on Monday, Tuesday, and Wednesday (with the Par-3 Contest Wednesday morning) followed by the actual tournament Thursday through Sunday. An even bigger dream would come true. Our plan was for Ben and me to fly south on Sunday evening (staying again in Aiken) and catch the action Monday through Thursday. Lindsey, Jeanine, Greta (almost four), and Ellie (eighteen months) would fly there Thursday night so we could take turns going to the tournament on Friday through Sunday.

Ben and I rolled into Aiken at 3:00 AM Monday. After a few hours' sleep, we arose so we could get to the course early. Our friend Guy Paradise had obtained tickets for Monday and Tuesday; we met him and enjoyed the day together. Storms rolled in, and all patrons were cleared from the course at 3:00 PM. The rain continued into Tuesday, so the course didn't open until 12:45; the line was long for patrons to re-enter the course, so we didn't get in until 2:00. That afternoon we watched from various vantage points. We sat in the stands by the No. 16 (par 3) tee box and laughed and cheered with the crowds who were watching golfers try to skip their tee shots across the full length of the pond onto the green (a Masters practice-round tradition). Guy and I had agreed to meet under the oak tree by the clubhouse at 3:00. I got a late start from No. 16 and knew I had to hurry. At one point, I broke into an easy jog, and I had only run a few steps before a marshal spotted me and told me to walk. I arrived late and missed Guy. He had waited a few minutes and then taken off. Without cell phones and with so many people, it's nearly impossible to coordinate meetings.

Ben and I watched the Par 3 Contest almost sitting on No. 4 green. Golfers (Jack Nicklaus is on the right) putted out just a few feet from us.

The Par 3 Contest on Wednesday was the highlight of the pre-tournament action. We arrived early so that we could scope out good seats and chose to sit greenside on No. 4. Golfers hit their tee shots right at us. The golf balls, tiny white dots in the blue sky, would plop down only a few yards away. There were three holes-in-one during the Par 3 Contest. Mark O'Meara holed out on No. 5, right after we saw him putt out on No. 4. There was a loud roar from the green, so we knew someone had put one in the cup. Shane Lowry and Matt Wallace also hit holes-in-one.

Our plans changed as we neared the weekend. An April snowstorm descended upon St. Paul on Thursday. Jeanine made it there from Rochester, but the flight (to Charleston, North Carolina, from the Twin Cities) was delayed until late in the evening. To make matters worse, Ellie had come down with something "croup-like" and was not feeling well. Lindsey wasn't sure if they should come given the weather and Ellie's health. But they changed their flight to one leaving on Friday and arrived around suppertime Friday night. The delays due to the weather and Ellie's health were troubling for Ben and me, so it took some of the fun and excitement out of our Thursday and Friday at the Masters.

Jeanine and I were sitting at one of these tables sipping an Azalea cocktail with Jon Rahm's future in-laws when Tiger sank his winning putt.

Ben and Linds attended the tournament on Saturday while Jeanine and I stayed in Aiken with the girls. Poor Ellie was not herself. She was trying to be good but was just out of sorts. It was a long day. Jeanine and I were there Sunday for one of the most memorable Masters final rounds of all time. Because of the threat of thunderstorms, it began at 7:30 AM, earlier than usual, with threesomes rather than twosomes. We arrived midmorning, put our chairs on No. 15 fairway, and then headed to behind the green on the par 4 No. 7 to watch the action. The first group we saw included Justin Thomas, Phil Mickelson, and Jon Rahm, and then we watched five more. The last threesome included Francisco Molinari (who was then leading), Tony Finau, and Tiger Woods. Molinari bogeyed the hole and Tiger hit his approach shot to within six inches of the cup and tapped it in for a birdie, so he gained two strokes on Molinari. From No. 7, we hustled over to our chairs on No. 15 (par 5). This would be the hole where Tiger emerged as the leader. Molinari had hit his ball into the water on No. 12. On No. 15, he laid up short of the green. His approach shot clipped a tree and landed in the water in front of the green. He would bogey the hole. Tiger drove the green in two and two-putted for a birdie to gain two strokes. As Tiger, Molinari, and Finau walked to the par 3, No. 16 tee box, I headed toward the No. 16 green. I couldn't get close, but I did hear (feel) the roar as Tiger's ball curled close to the hole.

Jeanine and I began walking from No. 15 back to the No. 18 green. The area was so packed with patrons that we decided to sit and sip an Azalea cocktail on the patio outside the clubhouse. The umbrellaed tables seated six. We spotted one that had a couple seated at it, and they welcomed us to join them. We struck up a conversation and learned that they were the parents of Jon Rahm's fiancé. She and Jon had met during their college years at Arizona State, and they were to be married in November. Rahm had been paired with Tiger on Thursday and Friday of the tournament, and he finished in a tie for ninth. The crowd let out a tremendous roar when Tiger rolled in his winning two-foot putt. He raised his arms in joy and, on his way to the clubhouse through the throng of people, stopped to hug his mom, girlfriend, and children, Charlie and Sam. Woods had won his fifth Masters title, and fifteenth major, by one stroke ahead of three runners-up. It left him one shy of Jack Nicklaus's record six Masters wins, and three short of Nicklaus's record of eighteen major wins. At age forty-three, Woods became the second oldest Masters winner, again only bettered by Nicklaus, who won at age forty-six. Because of the high profile of Woods and his storied fall from the top of the game due to personal issues and injuries, the victory generated a large amount of publicity around the world and is regarded as one of the best comebacks in all of sports. And just think, we were there to be part of it!

I find it hard to believe that Jeanine and I were at the Masters on Sunday to see Tiger's come-from-behind win.

THE OLDER I GET THE BETTER I WAS

Family Golf Memories
When Sue lived in Scottsdale, Arizona, she and her husband, Dan, were members of Troon North Golf Club, and we golfed there several times. Jeanine will never let me forget the day I golfed wearing her Liz Claiborne shorts. I had black golfing shorts that looked much like hers. When I woke up to head out to the course with Dad and Dan, I grabbed what I thought were my golf shorts from the ironing board, put them on, and off we went. I was on the driving range hitting a few balls before our round began when Jeanine and Sue drove by. Jeanine was laughing at my wardrobe gaffe, which I had not yet realized. I didn't play well that day, and I've always attributed it to my attire!

Sue and Dan divorced in 1995. A few years later she met Dudley Merkel, another fine person and avid golfer. They were members of the Desert Highlands Golf Club where we golfed, dined, and enjoyed the impressive eighteen-hole putting green. Friends of Sue and Dudley belonged to the Desert Mountain Golf Club where The Tradition tournament was held for players on the Champions Tour (for PGA golfers fifty and older). Through that connection, we attended The Tradition several times. Sue and Dudley moved to Flagstaff, Arizona, and eventually had homes in Flagstaff and Sedona, so with them we golfed at Forest Highlands (Flagstaff), the Sedona public course (breathtaking), and Seven Canyons (where Dudley worked at the time in sales).

One of Dudley's best friends is PGA golfer Tom Weiskopf. Weiskopf turned professional in 1964 and played on the PGA Tour for many years before going on the Champions Tour. He won sixteen PGA Tour titles between 1968 and 1982; his most successful decade was the 1970s. His top finishes in the major tournaments included winning The Open Championship in 1973, placing second at The Masters four times (1969, 1972, 1974, and 1975), placing second in the U.S. Open in 1976, and finishing third in the PGA Championship in 1973. Dudley and his wife before Sue lived next door to the Weiskopfs in a Forest Highlands villa in Flagstaff. They became friends and remained so in the years that followed. We had opportunities to visit with Tom several times during our trips to see Sue and Dudley. I don't recall the year, but it was a March visit because Tom and I were sitting in Sue's living room watching the Final Four basketball tournament. Tom is a tall man, 6 feet 3 inches, and he had a reputation for a terrible temper when he played on tour (they called him "the towering inferno"), but off the course he was as pleasant as could be. For several years after Mom died, Dad spent a few months during the winter with Sue and Dudley. During these stays, he got to visit with Tom, and they became good friends. One spring, Tom was going to play in a Champion's Tour event on the outskirts of Minneapolis. He brought Dad with him on his private jet, which was especially generous of him. I recall picking Dad up at the Humphrey Airport (now Terminal 2). Dad confirmed that private jetting was a grand way to travel.

The Veterans Memorial Golf Club in Clear Lake is a nine-hole vacation course. I've golfed hundreds of rounds there with Dad, Ben, Jeanine, Sue, my cousins, Uncle Ross, all four of Sue's husbands and significant others (Randy Budihas, Dan Harris, Dudley Merkle, and Tom Hendricks), Dad's friend Harry Bovaird, and many more. Though Clear Lake's course doesn't hold a candle to Augusta, Troon North, Forest Highlands, or Seven Canyons, my memories of golfing there are as meaningful and intense as my memories of golfing anywhere else.

Dad golfed into his mid-eighties. I can see him bending down to tee up his ball. His hand shakes a bit as he places the ball on the tee. He's cut a few fingers from his golf glove to make room for his arthritically swollen hands. He addresses the ball, slides his driver back and forth away from him a few times behind the tee, takes his arms back (but his shoulders don't turn, as is often the case with senior golfers), and then gives the ball a solid whack. His ball slices, starting out left and circling back to land somewhere in the fairway a hundred and fifty yards or so out. The shots that followed were often plentiful and diverse. Dad put a suction cup on the end of his putter so he could retrieve his putts from the cup without bending over. Through the years, he "owned" the par 5 No. 8. He sometimes birdied it when we played and often made par. All it took was one good hole to make the round a fun one for him. Dad died in 2016 at age ninety-three. I'd give anything to be able to play another nine holes with him.

Bicycling
A ride where I almost bought the farm

With Ben in Burlington after completing the seven-day, four hundred forty-five-mile bicycle ride across Iowa (RAGBRAI) in 2009

My bicycle gave me the same sense of freedom in my childhood years that driving a car did later on. It got me from point A to point B nicely, from our house to my friends' (Bill Farnan and Joe Jensen) houses, only a block away, to Lincoln School playground for pickup softball games, to downtown Clear Lake to shop at Satter's Sporting Goods or sip a cherry coke at the Corner Drug Store, and to my grandparents' farm a mile south of town. I had a transistor radio in a brown leather case about the size of a pack of cigarettes that I would hang from my handlebars so I could listen to Mason City's KRIB, a rock station, or KGLO, which broadcast Minnesota Twins games (but otherwise played music for old folks). Some days I'd bike with friends along gravel country roads looking for pop bottles that could be cashed in for five or ten cents each at Foodland, our neighborhood grocery store.

On my bike, age five, with no idea of the many miles I would ride in my life

In my first two years of college at Iowa State University, my bike was my main means of transportation. One day I was pedaling home past some shops to my dorm about a mile south of campus. As I passed a car that had stopped in traffic, a woman in the front passenger seat opened her door in front of me. I crashed into the door and came to an immediate stop. She looked angrily at me, as if I had done something wrong, and got out of the car, and then her husband drove away. In a few seconds, my front tire blew with a loud BANG and went flat, and I stood there thinking "What the heck just happened?" I walked my bike to the dorm and from that day on kept a wary eye out for car doors that might open in front of me.

Within a year or two of moving to Rochester, I bought a really nice bike. I can't recall the brand (it was French made, maybe a Peugeot) or where I purchased it, but it was bright white and wonderfully lightweight. I started taking long bike rides with Greg Caucutt and other friends. Rochester sponsored a one-hundred-mile ride, the Centurion, that first headed southwest of town and then north and east through Plainview and back to Rochester on County Road 9. There were rest stops about every twenty-five miles. I have badges for completing the ride in 1972, 1973, 1974, 1977, 1982, and 1983. In 1972, the ride was on or near my birthday (July 30). Jeanine biked seventy-five miles that day on her yellow Schwinn and then took the sag wagon home to bake my birthday cake and prepare dinner for me, Mom, and Dad. Always good with artistic endeavors, Jeanine made a bicycle out of plastic-wrapped wire for the cake decoration.

Bicycling Across Iowa
RAGBRAI is an acronym for the Register's Annual Great Bicycle Ride Across Iowa, a noncompetitive ride organized by *The Des Moines Register*. The ride goes across the state annually from west to east and draws riders from across the United States and many foreign countries. RAGBRAI is the largest bike-touring event in the world. Riders begin at a community on Iowa's western border and ride to a community on the eastern border, stopping in towns across the state. The ride is one week long, ending on the last Saturday of July each year, after beginning on the previous Sunday. The earliest possible starting date is July 19 and the latest is July 25.

RAGBRAI began in 1973 when *Des Moines Register* feature writers John Karras and Donald Kaul decided to go on a bicycle ride across the state. Both men were avid cyclists. Karras challenged Kaul to do the ride and write articles about what he experienced. Kaul agreed, but only if Karras also did the ride, so Karras then agreed to ride as well. (Kaul had a daily column in the *Register* that I loved to read. When I went to college, Mom clipped and saved his articles for me.) The newspaper's management approved of the plan. Don Benson, a public relations director at the *Register*, was assigned to coordinate the event. At the suggestion of Ed Heins, the managing editor, the writers invited the public to accompany them. The ride was planned to start on August 26 in Sioux City and end in Davenport on August 31. The overnight stops were Storm Lake, Fort Dodge, Ames, Des Moines, and Williamsburg. The *Register* informed readers of the event as well as the planned route. The ride was informally referred to as The Great Six-Day Bicycle Ride.

Some three hundred cyclists began the ride in Sioux City; one hundred and fourteen of them rode the entire route and the rest part of the route. Attendance was light the first year, probably because the event was announced with only six weeks' notice and also conflicted with the first week of school and the final weekend of the Iowa State Fair.

After the ride was over, Kaul and Karras wrote numerous articles that captured the imaginations of many readers. Among those who completed the 1973 ride was eighty-three-year-old Clarence Pickard of Indianola. He rode a used ladies' Schwinn and wore a long-sleeved shirt, trousers, woolen long underwear, and a silver pith helmet. He said that the underwear blocked out the sun and kept his skin cool. The newspaper received many calls and letters from people who wanted to go on the ride but had been unable to for various reasons. Because of this public response and demand, a second ride was scheduled for the next year, 1974, from August 4 to 10, before the Iowa State Fair.

The length of the entire week's route averages four hundred and sixty-eight miles; the miles-per-day average is sixty-eight. Eight host communities are selected each year, one each for the beginning and end points and the other six serving as overnight stops from Sunday through Friday for the bicyclists. At the beginning of the ride, participants have traditionally dipped the rear wheels of their bikes in water in or near the starting community. A dipping spot has always been set up in either the Missouri River or Big Sioux River. At the end, the riders dip the front wheels in the Mississippi River.

I didn't ride in my first RAGBRAI until 2008, the year I turned sixty. It was Ben's idea to do so. We rode the first half (from Missouri Valley to Ames) and had a blast. We were hooked. (Jeanine drove from town to town to provide sag wagon support and would do so on all of

THE OLDER I GET THE BETTER I WAS

2008 RAGBRAI:
In Ames, Iowa

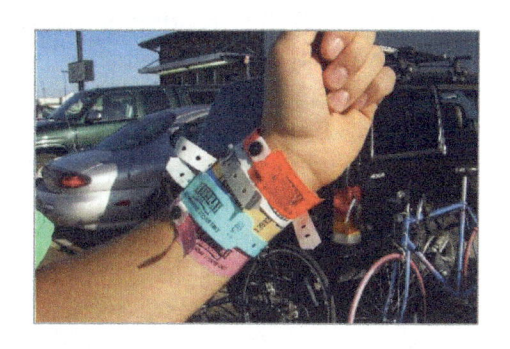

2009 RAGBRAI: Daily wristbands

2010 RAGBRAI, day 3: Lindsey, Ben, Randy, me

2011 RAGBRAI, day 1: Randy, Ben, Lindsey, Caitlin, me

2014 RAGBRAI: Sue, Ben, Jeanine, Lindsey

our RAGBRAIs.) Lindsey joined us in 2009. She was able to ride the first four days, from Council Bluffs to Chariton, and then left to join her family in Okoboji for her grandfather's funeral. Ben and I rode on to the end in Burlington. We expanded our group for the 2010 RAGBRAI to include my cousin Randy from Wheeling, West Virginia. That ride began in Sioux City and ended in Dubuque. Jeanine provided sag wagon support in the veggie fuel–powered bus we drove. Summit, Ben and Lindsey's trusty dog, came along, too. The bus broke down, conveniently, in Clear Lake, the halfway stopping point for the ride. We were able to find and rent another van so we could keep on trucking. In 2011, the group expanded again to include Randy's wife, Robin, and Caitlin Grom, a friend of Ben and Lindsey. Robin and Jeanine provided sag wagon support. Summit came along, too. This ride, which began in Glenwood and ended in Davenport, was a grueling one. It was extremely hot all week. Some nights it was ninety degrees when we retired to our tents. The heat, humidity, and hills got to me about twenty miles from the finish on our first day. Ben called Jeanine and Robin to come and get me. This was the first time I recall not finishing an athletic event that I had started. Fortunately, I recovered after a good night's rest and carried on without incident the rest of the ride. Randy crashed at midweek and was cut and bruised but luckily did not break any bones. He, too, carried on after a night's rest. In 2014, Ben, Lindsey, and I biked a partial RAGBRAI because the route came through Clear Lake. We started in Forest City and ended in Waverly.

Following are a few notes and pictures from the 2009 and 2011 RAGBRAIs that provide a taste of the week-long experience.

2009 RAGBRAI: Council Bluffs to Burlington (445 miles)
The team: Ben, Lindsey, Jeanine, and me

July 18, Council Bluffs
We meet in Clear Lake at 4:00, drive two cars to Des Moines, leave Ben's Jeep at the Des Moines Hampton Inn, and then head to Council Bluffs in the Cherokee. We arrive at 8:30 PM. Tents are everywhere as far as the eye can see. Our hotel is right at the center of the action. We check in and then stroll over to Rib Fest to enjoy a beautiful evening.

THE OLDER I GET THE BETTER I WAS

The band Bare Naked Ladies plays on stage. Ben and Lindsey ride the Xtracycle. We're anxious to get RAGBRAI underway and are wide-eyed at the sight of so many cyclists, team buses, and tents.

Day 1: Council Bluffs to Red Oak 
Jeanine, Lindsey, and I begin our daily morning routine of studying the map to determine how far it is between each rest stop, how far to the lunch stop, and how far to the destination town. We peer at the squiggly-lined elevation map to see where the steep hills will be. (We never did figure out how to predict the big hills.) Jeanine has a different challenge each morning in finding what roads will lead to the lunch town. Ben, on the other hand, has no time for maps or checkpoints. Hills bother him not, nor do distances. He is, however, particular about the pressure in his pink-tired Trek, so while he pumps, Lindsey, Jeanine, and I pore over the maps.

We peddle east out of Council Bluffs around 8:15 on a blue-sky, bright-sun morning and delight in a relatively flat, light-wind-at-the-back ride. On a scale of one to ten, this ride is a ten. During the day, an ambulance or two flies by, sirens blaring—a reminder of the biking dangers. We arrive in Red Oak at 2:30. We couldn't have had a nicer day to begin RAGBRAI with a positive, confidence-building experience. We dine at Johnny's Steak House, the best restaurant of the whole week. Spaghetti never tasted better.

Day 2: Red Oak to Greenfield 
The real biking test begins today. We face the most vertical climb of any RAGBRAI day (5,096 feet) and a seventy-five-mile ride. The wind is light but out of the south and southeast, so it will not be our friend. The first half is tough, especially the hills. A light

rain begins to fall as we ride into Corning, our meeting town. While Jeanine and Ben get lunch, Lindsey and I talk about the ride so far. She says she's thinking of riding the rest of way with Jeanine, that maybe she's had enough for today. It's been a tough morning. I tell her I wouldn't blame her for ending now and starting strong tomorrow. When Ben returns, however, he will hear nothing of the sort. "You'll regret it," he says, "for not going all the way. Come on, tough it out; you can do it." And do it Lindsey does! We finish feeling pretty good; we passed our test! Ate tasty pasta at the Greenfield Hotel. Ben shops for old camera equipment at an antique store. We take over the entire B&B basement.

Day 3: Greenfield to Indianola

A grueling day. We're looking at seventy-seven miles with 4,470 feet of climb. We get a late start from the B&B, around 9:30 AM. It's cloudy and sixty-three degrees. There are longer-than-usual gaps between rest stops (thirteen, fourteen, and sixteen miles). Ben continues to get a lot of compliments on his pink tires. Both he and Lindsey are biking strong. Our lunch town, St. Charles, is fifty miles—a long way—into the ride. After lunch, the sky clears, and a beautiful afternoon and evening unfold. Dinner in Indianola. The Fat Tires go down smooth.

Meeting Towns

RAGBRAI calls them meeting towns. We call them lunch stops. They're towns somewhere near the midpoint of each day's ride in which vendors serve brats, burgers, gyros, corn on the cob, turkey legs, ice cream, pie, and all sorts of energy-replenishing foods. There are hundreds if not thousands of bikers milling about each town when we arrive. We bike into the crowd, then have to hop off and walk our bikes while we walkie-talkie Jeanine to see where she might be. (Bikers had cell phones, but phone service could not handle the sea of bikers.) Hearing her cheerful voice always perks us up. We can't wait to collapse into the pink, blue, and red lawn chairs that she has set up and are waiting for us. Nothing feels as good as easing a tired body into one of those chairs, munching on a sandwich, sipping a Mountain Dew, and just watching the bikers all around us. We eat, but it seems we never get full, as if we're feeding bottomless pits. Each day we believe if we can make it to the meeting town in good shape, the rest of the ride will be a snap. We owe Jeanine a huge thanks for being the best sag-wagoner in all of RAGBRAI.

Day 4: Indianola to Chariton
A fairly easy day—flat terrain, relatively cool, and not many miles. We need a less taxing day after yesterday and before our hundred-miler tomorrow. After the ride, we drive to Indianola to pick up Ben's Jeep, which we had parked at the home of Jennifer Sorensen's brother. We can't find a good restaurant on the return; we're looking for that elusive Olive Garden, which isn't to be found in southern Iowa. We settle for Old Milwaukees in a busy Chariton bar and vendor food in the city park. We have only one room at the Super 8, the "smoking queen" as we call it, so Ben and Lindsey tent in town. Around 2:00 AM a crash-banging storm rolls through. They abandon the tent to sleep in the Jeep.

Day 5: Chariton to Ottumwa
Jeanine and I arrive at Ben and Lindsey's campsite. He is sleeping in the Jeep; she is snoozing in the tent. We say our goodbyes to Lindsey, who leaves for her family gathering and grandfather's memorial service in Okoboji. She has done remarkably well, and we're sad she can't stay for the entire ride. So, after a night in which Ben has had little rest, he and I saddle up, and we try not to think about the hundred miles facing us. We take the Karras Loop near the middle of the ride, which takes us around Rathbun Lake and adds the necessary mileage to get us over the one-hundred-mile mark for the day. We grind it out. On the way into Ottumwa, we see storm clouds in the offing. It's raining where we're headed (and where Jeanine is finding

us a room at the wonderful Ottumwa Hotel) but not where we are. It seems to take forever to bike the last few miles. We stop and have our picture taken by another biker. His odometer shows the hundred miles logged during the day. We spot Jeanine near "tent city," and she whisks us to our hotel, where we have a fine dinner and a restful evening.

Day 6: Ottumwa to Mount Pleasant

We leave Ottumwa around 8:30 AM, biking up a long, steep hill to get out of town. Yesterday's route, because of its length, was the toughest of the ride. Today, though it has the flattest terrain of the ride, is the second toughest because of the heat, humidity, and strong winds from the south and southeast. Plus, there are few clouds to hide the hot sun, and it's a long way, about fifty-two miles, to Brighton, our lunch town.

I am gassed at Brighton. Ben's biking strong, as if he could continue on for days without a break. But after lunch, I regroup and hang in there. We see one biker down on the highway; his neck is in a brace and he's being lifted onto a stretcher. Two other bikers collide and fall at the "welcome finish" in Mount Pleasant. We meet Jeanine at the gyro tent in Mount Pleasant's Central Park.

Day 7: Mount Pleasant to Burlington

One couldn't have scripted a better final day for our first border-to-border RAGBRAI. On our way at 8:15. Storms came through at night, which lowered the heat and humidity. We peddle along flat highways under blue skies in cool temps, flying along with a tailwind from the northwest. A biker's heaven. We zip to the first town in an incredibly short time. I ride along looking around, trying to soak in all the experiences and memories from the week. One doesn't get to accomplish many firsts like this. I felt so alive, so lucky to be healthy enough to do this with Ben, Jeanine, and Lindsey. Memories I will treasure as long as I live.

THE OLDER I GET THE BETTER I WAS

Each day was a new adventure, with new towns, terrain, weather, and places to stay. I don't want the week to end.

A surprise as we enter Burlington, and the ride ends. It's Snake Alley, a winding, steep uphill climb with a pitch like Lombard Street in San Francisco. Ben lets me go first, which I appreciate, and he and I wind our way to the top without a hint of having to stop and walk. From there we bike slowly along residential streets to the Mississippi, There, along with hundreds if not thousands of other bikers, we dip our front wheels in the river and have our picture taken. From there, we jump in the Cherokee with Jeanine and drive back to Clear Lake. RAGBRAI 2009 is over. We did it!

RAGBRAI 2011 Ramblings: Glenwood to Davenport (455 miles)
The team: Ben, Lindsey, Randy and Robin Forzano, Caitlin Grom, Summit, Jeanine, and me

Glenwood
First night with Craig and Teresa, our home hosts. Rainbow upon driving to town. Winery. Owner brought Summit through the restaurant to outdoor patio and fed him French fries. Cheese plate. Super breakfast. Tab explosion in the trailer.
Day 1: Glenwood to Atlantic (63.8 miles)
Observed dispute between bikers because lady wouldn't pay for a bent bike wheel. **Carson** (meeting town without Jeanine and Robin). Traffic jam first day. Ate gyros by dumpster. Mike begins to cramp in a Mountain Dew daze. Photos by town hall. Smoothies. Bridesmaid invitation after lunch stop. **Griswold.** Foreshadow of future events. Mike's meltdown in spite of pickle and banana. Joyce helps with basement arrangement. **Lewis.** Big bike town. Young Minnesota lad who was left behind by his family. Didn't know about sag wagon. (Family went on RAGBRAI without knowing what it was. "Griswolds go on RAGBRAI.") Outspoken South Dakota lady. **Atlantic.** Sitting in Ralph's front yard with his family and friends. Mexican restaurant. Ate our whole meal without silverware. Ultra Girl night. Caitlin's sunburn comes alive. Wal-Mart run with Jeanine to buy leggings for Caitlin (they only had black). Cicada on Lindsey's bike. Pole dancers cancel on

Ralph. His main bathroom is in his basement. Ralph's Minnesota and Iowa jokes. Ralph's warning: "Watch out for critters in the backyard."

Day 2: Atlantic to Carroll (65.8 miles)
We got lost leaving **Atlantic**. Lindsey, Randy, Caitlin go one way; Mike and Ben go another. Caitlin's lowest moment. Ben has to sit by the Viking to wait for the others. Lots of hills, heat, humidity. Windmill. Danish. Banana crepes. Photos with mannequin (creepy Viking guy) sitting on bench. Young high school girls as mermaids. Randy: "That is not appropriate." Free beer coins for establishment yet to be built. Handing out utensils—Ben grabs—because you never know when we'd need them. **Manning.** Ethan, a triplet, in big trouble, gone from home too long. Randy and Jeanine seesaw. She in sports outfit. Robin singing with the band. Ben in conference call; did not get fired. Brats, pizza, maze, and barn. **Templeton.** Templeton Rye whiskey. Cars made of wood. Very hot. Condom queen. Young buck forfeits condom to Ben, which later sticks on his shirt. Orange crush bikes are best friends forever. Symbolic. Ben goes uphill twice in a failed attempt to get free beer. **Wiley.** Watermelon. Huge hill entering town. Loud announcer. Jeanine and Robin floor it over the boulders. **Carroll.** Stayed with Penny, Ed, Terry, and Joyce. Slept in lower level. Air conditioned. Ben slept outside with Summit. Very efficient shower plan that night. Chocolate chip muffins. Dinner at the Winery. Great food, good waitress, weird ropes everywhere in the dining area. Summit stayed in car. Wine tasting. Bought a bottle of wine.

Day 3: Carroll to Boone (100-mile day for Ben and Lindsey; 71.5 miles for others)
Lidderdale. Caitlin has chain problem. Lindsey drafts behind Michigan Ultra group. A good morning. **Lanesboro.** Lindsey has to wait forever by post office. Lindsey's chain comes off at bottom of hill. **Churdan** (meeting town). Peanut-butter-and-jelly-sandwich day on lady's lawn. Memorial park. Randy crashes bike after lunch but bravely survives, almost unscathed. He and Mike go to police officer for first aid. Officer is able to be helpful even though he just shot and killed someone a few days earlier. Ben and Lindsey get separated again. Ben and Lindsey eat at PB&J stand. So do Caitlin, Randy, and Mike, who

buys bracelet for J9. Hopes of Team B (Caitlin, Randy, and Mike) beating Lindsey to Boone are crushed (the former biking 70+ miles, the latter 100). **Dana.** Karras loop badge stop. Lindsey makes it before Ben. **Pilot Mound.** Team B meets up with Lindsey and Ben. Lindsey gets "hit on" by man on street watching bikers go by: "I like the way your frame is put together." Buttons. Twister Hill. Twelve-year-old photographs Jake the Snake (Caitlin's borrowed bike). Beers without Randy at the farm after Twister Hill. (Randy had biked on.) Mike's bike stolen temporarily. He was too dazed to realize it was right where he left it. **Boone.** Tented near a Little League baseball park. Best concession stand dinner ever. Showered by hosing off near the stand during the game. Homeless guy. Randy's outlook for the rest of RAGBRAI is bleak. Fat Tire taste testing.

Day 4: Boone to Altoona (54.9 miles)
Luther. Thought it was going to rain, but it didn't. Mike's red bike helmet begins to turn pink from sun's heat. **Slater.** Ben and Lindsey beat Team Escort to town. Caitlin rides with Bad Boys. **Sheldahl.** Roof Brain marketing maintains steady pace. **Alleman.** No beer in town. Church has sign "Lance Armstrong Is Not Here." **White Oak.** White Oak Winery. Ben and Lindsey pictured with pig bus at Winery. **Bondurant.** Lindsey and Ben have tallboys at Casey's. Randy, Caitlin, and Mike stop for margaritas. **Altoona.** Olive Garden dinner. Waiter Rolando, who Randy calls "Jorge." Stay with Deckers. English village with guest house (i.e., compound). Jeanine and Robin suffering from heat stroke. Bathtubs and showers rusty. 93 degrees at midnight. Rolando offers us his place; we almost take it. Van clicker almost doesn't work. Summit inside, van running with air conditioning on.

Day 5: Altoona to Grinnell (56.2 miles)
Sixty-six hill countdown. (There were sixty-six hills in this 56.2 mile stretch. After the first hill, there was a sign saying, "only sixty-five more to go." Signs counted down until the last one.) **Mitchellville** (lunch town). Skipped because such a short ride. **Colfax.** Spun the wheel at Casey's. Ben won a cake donut. Mike won a beach ball. Lindsey won pizza. Randy won a donut. Caitlin got a water. Ben finds a bike admirer, a Trek distributor. Ate lunch on the corner. Big hill out of town with

the beer cup obstacle course. Jeanine and Robin trapped at top of hill in the van. Backing-up problem. Looped through water towers and moved water stations in order to get out. Lindsey gets cheered up the hill as "Whitey." **Baxter.** Caitlin encounters bikers who had just visited adult porn shop. Biker asks her, "Want to touch my boobs?" Caitlin does. We bike under Interstate 80 for the fiftieth time (it seems). **Rock Creek State Park.** Stopped by lake for nachos and cheese. Randy, Caitlin, and Mike are recruited into the Marines. They then bike twenty-one miles nonstop. Finally, not as hot. **Grinnell.** Listen to band, Tang. New tires and alignment for our vehicle at Al's. Air-conditioned house. Palin's movie *Undefeated*. Creepy neighbor. Marijuana plant in backyard. Black undies in the laundry. Mexican place for dinner. Terrible bartender; didn't know jack. Left to go to steak house. Salad bar guy (old guy in biker shorts and shirt, large butt and belly). Long wait to check out. Computer breaks, no bill, but we pay anyway. Banana man vehicle sighting. Guy from Altoona greets biker with flag and appears later in ride.

Day 6: Grinnell to Coralville (76.0 miles)
Brooklyn. Town of flags. Free bloodies with $4 cup. Screwdrivers. Breakfast sandwiches. Caitlin rides in with the Bad Boys. **Victor.** Randy, Caitlin, and Mike have Constitutional lesson on the road. **Ladora.** Randy thought it to be creepy. **Marengo.** Lunch town. Walked around looking for corn on the cob. Dancing in the park. **West Amana.** Barn tour for Robin and Jeanine for RASVAI (Registers Annual Support Vehicle Across Iowa.) **South Amana.** Ben and Lindsey stop at general store. Caitlin, Randy, and Mike do the extra loop (a few more blocks). Lots of traffic both ways on the road. Dust in our eyes. **Oxford.** Cool bed and breakfasts. Snickers on the hill. **Coralville.** Randy, Mike, and Caitlin take the scenic route to house. Blue-eyed Owen (son of guest of host family). Scott gives us corn on the cob. Summit had a dog encounter through the fence. Los Potriolos for dinner for Mike's birthday eve. Steve, Jennifer, Kevin, and Liz join us. Rum and Cokes. Jeanine's water margarita. Ben's two plate–special dinner. Sombrero with tequila shot under the bright lights for Mike. Good sleep but ground wet.

THE OLDER I GET THE BETTER I WAS

Day 7 and Mike's Birthday: Coralville to Davenport (64.6 miles)
Ben loses shoes temporarily. Scott notices Randy's bike's front wheel isn't screwed in (saves life). **Iowa City.** Hill in campus a mini killer. Pretty campus. Mike kept thinking it was a 54-mile day, rather than a 64.6. **West Branch.** Ben and Lindsey have Bloody Marys, biscuits, and gravy. **Springdale.** Caitlin, Randy, and Mike meet up with Ben and Lindsey. **Moscow.** Turkey Toms for Caitlin, Randy, and Mike. **Wilton.** Ben and Lindsey have 32 oz. of High Life and Pizza at the Kwik Trip. **Durant.** Quick water stop with Cokes. Lady with microphone announces fresh fruit. **Walcott.** Blew through. **Davenport.** Deceiving mile signs. Penny farthing bike. Reroute because of early running race. Mississippi River. Photo of us taken by us with man wearing necklace with lady flashing boobs. McDonalds for dinner. Long, safe trip home during which we log the following memories, which Caitlin appropriately titles "RAGGIEs:"

RAGGIEs (our best and worst awards)
- Best dinner: Olive Garden
- Best host: Ralph
- Best overnight: Henry's house
- Best riding day: Thursday
- Worst hill: Twister Hill
- Best lunch stop: Manning (Ethan and seesawing in park)
- Best route town: Brooklyn
- Worst day: Tuesday (Karras hundred-mile loop and Randy's crash day)
- Best lunch food: Gyros
- Best beverage: Fat Tire
- Best giveaway: Fat Tire stuff, Frisbee and Chapstick
- Best costume: Loin cloth guy
- Best team name: Bikesexuals
- Best comeback: Tie Randy and Mike
- Best virgin: Cat Black
- Best bathroom: Craig and Teresa's
- Worst bathroom: Dee Decker farm

- Most speedy: Ben
- Fastest Centurion: Lindsey
- Best team player: Robin
- Best overnight town: Grinnell
- Biggest granddaughter: Brenda
- Best mascot: Summit
- Favorite kid: Ethan
- Worst bartender: Mexican restaurant guy
- Best waiter: Rolando and wine-tasting lady
- Best bus driver: Jeanine
- Best snoring: Jeanine
- Best song: "Down, Down, Do Your Thing"
- Funniest moment: Mike, Randy, and Caitlin looking for Randy and Caitlin
- Best moment: Mike's sombrero birthday celebration
- Best photo: Mike taking a shot
- Best snack on the go: Carrot Cake Cliff Bar
- Worst sunburn: Caitlin and Lindsey
- Worst smell: Scott's home's lower level

    I'm not sure why I didn't ride RAGBRAI in the 1970s. I think my reason was that I had only two weeks' vacation (three weeks starting in 1975) and I didn't want to use so many days of it on biking. Jeanine and I discovered Aspen, Colorado, in the early 1970s, and we loved it so much that our vacationing there took priority. The last week in July will always make me think of RAGBRAI fun.

    When I biked my first RAGBRAI in 2008, when I turned sixty, I thought I was pretty old. I realize now how young I really was. I'm not sure if I have another full-week RAGBRAI in me; I know I can't handle the high heat and humidity. The good news is that all the miles I've biked over the years (since that picture of me in front of my house on the bike with training wheels) are on my permanent record; they can't ever be taken away.

    In addition to organized, many-bikers rides like RAGBRAI and Rochester's Centurion, I often rode on shorter rides with fewer people.

THE OLDER I GET THE BETTER I WAS

Jeanine and I loved biking the Sparta-to-Elroy trail in Wisconsin, on thirty-three miles of railroad track that had been converted to a crushed rock trail. It is acknowledged to be the oldest rail–trail conversion in the United States. Bikers pass through three hand-dug railroad tunnels. Two are sixteen hundred feet long and the other is thirty-eight hundred feet. They are unlit, and water drips down the walls and pools at your feet. The temperature in the tunnels is a cool fifty to sixty degrees, regardless of the outside temperature. We also biked the Rochester-to–Pine Island trail (twenty-five miles round trip) dozens of times over the years, always looking forward to a stop at the Pine Island Cheese Mart to rest before our ride home. Greg Caucutt, Fred Huss, and I one year biked from Rochester to Eau Claire (Greg's

With cousin Randy Forzano in the 1970s. Biking was just one of several sports he and I have enjoyed over the years.

hometown, about one hundred miles away) one way and were picked up by our wives. The wind was at our backs the entire trip, a biker's paradise. Greg and I biked from Clear Lake to Rochester one summer (about ninety miles). On our ride home, passing a farmhouse, two snarling dogs came charging out after us. The farmer with them said, "My dog won't hurt you, but I don't know about that other dog (the bigger one). I don't know who he belongs to." When the dogs charged, Greg and I dismounted and walked. The stray dog was calm when we walked, but the minute we started to get on and ride, he would growl and bark. The dog's head came up to the top crossbar of my bike. We walked probably a quarter of a mile before the dog lost interest and wandered off.

For many years, Rod Morlock organized a family and friends ride on Memorial Day weekend and a weekend in the fall. In 1991, he and I planned a bicycling and baseball weekend with our families, Greg Caucutt, and Keith Fisher. We biked about sixty miles on the Cedar Valley Nature Trail from its start near Waterloo, Iowa, to Cedar

Rapids. That evening, we attended the Cedar Rapids Kernels Minor League baseball game. The Kernels pitcher and shortstop, Trevor Hoffman, played for them that season. Hoffman could throw in the mid-nineties, and he was attracting a lot of interest. There were several major league scouts behind home plate, their radar guns validating that Hoffman could really bring it. Just two year later, he began an eighteen-year career as a major league relief pitcher, most of them with the San Diego Padres, and he was inducted into the Major League Baseball Hall of Fame in 2018. I remember watching the Kernels' fleet-footed left fielder, Motorboat (Eugene) Jones, who had one of my favorite baseball nicknames of all time. He made neither the majors nor the Hall of Fame.

Hiking
A premonition haunts a hike.

With Frank Earnest in 2016. We hiked across the Grand Canyon from North Rim to South, 23.9 miles, in two days.

Though I tried downhill skiing in Minnesota, I could not get the hang of it. I've never been one with a need for speed, and without lessons, I did not feel comfortable screaming down a snow-packed hill. When I thought of Aspen, Colorado, I thought of expensive mountain skiing and figured I didn't want any part of it. Shortly after Jeanine and I were married, she saw a magazine advertisement for.summer vacationing there. Lodging prices were much less than during the winter, the scenery was magnificent, hiking trails for all abilities were prevalent, and dining was delectable.

I credit Jeanine with discovering Aspen for summer hiking vacations. We traveled there often in the 1970s, and it became our all-time favorite summer getaway.

We made our first trip to Aspen in the summer of 1973 and immediately fell in love with it. It was the home of John Denver, Hunter Thompson, ski bums, hippies, music festivals, beautiful Victorian-style homes, incredibly well-conditioned bicycle riders, and lots of dogs. We rented a yellow, soft-topped CJ5 to do some off-roading and got hooked on that, too. (Soon after our return home, we bought a red, soft-topped CJ5, and since then there have been only a handful of years when we did not own at least one Jeep.) We found the perfect place to stay, the St. Moritz Lodge, just a few blocks from downtown. We walked everywhere and drove only to get to the hiking trails.

THE OLDER I GET THE BETTER I WAS

Aspen is where my love for hiking began. How sad Jeanine and I felt leaving after our first time there, seeing the mountains disappear in our rearview mirror as we headed east to Rochester. We came back in the summers of 1974, 1975, 1976, 1979, and 2013 (to celebrate forty years since our first visit).

The Grand Hike
I will be forever grateful to Frank Earnest for inviting me to hike with him across the Grand Canyon from North Rim to South. Following his and Sarah's move to Tucson, he joined a local hiking club and began trekking many trails in the area. In October 2015 he asked if I would be up to joining him on the Canyon hike. I had never seen the Grand Canyon, so I thought this would be a good chance to visit it and get a workout from hiking across it. Frank was super helpful. He made all of the arrangements and advised me on the hiking paraphernalia I should buy. I was in fairly good shape from my daily running, but a few months before the hike, I started walking briskly up and down the Ramsey Hill by the University Club nearly every visit to St. Paul. Here's how the Canyon hike is advertised:

> For the hearty souls who are willing to work for it, less than one percent of the Grand Canyon's five million annual visitors, the real magic lies below the rim. On this epic Grand Canyon hike, you'll leave from the North Kaibab Trail on the North Rim, challenging your personal limits as you descend 14.3 miles and 6,000 feet to the bottom of the canyon before connecting with the Bright Angel Trail and climbing 4,500 feet and 9.6 miles back out again to the South Rim.
>
> Along the North Kaibab Trail, you'll take in mesmerizing scenery as you pass through two billion years of the Earth's history and eleven layers of ancient rocks. Eventually, after hours of knee-pounding hiking, you'll reach the sandy banks of the Colorado River. Here, in the heart of the Grand Canyon National Park, dozens of massive rock formations will tower above you on all sides. For those with a love of the natural world, it's pure sensory overload—thrilling, dizzying, enlightening.
>
> At the bottom, you can enjoy a much-needed rest and overnight stay at Bright Angel Campground Phantom Ranch.
>
> Climbing out of the canyon along the Bright Angel Trail, considered to be the park's premiere trail, may be rewarding, but it's

no easy feat. However, ample shade, seasonal water sources, and views framed by massive cliffs make it a more pleasant, even enjoyable experience, for most hikers. Many, many switchbacks later when the journey is over, you'll stand along the top of the South Rim and know that you've seen the Grand Canyon in all of its glory.

Starting in mid-May, a week or two before the trip, I began to feel uneasy about the adventure. I appreciated Frank's trip preparations, and I knew I would be in capable hands with him if I needed medical assistance, but I began to worry about letting him down if for some reason I couldn't complete the hike. The only way out is by helicopter. I wondered how I would do with the heat at the canyon floor and then the climb out on day two. It was hard to train and prepare for those conditions in Rochester. Part of my trepidation came from not wanting to disrupt the routine that Jeanine and I enjoyed so much—coming to St. Paul each Thursday night to dine at a restaurant and stay at our condo, watching Greta and Ellie on Friday, going out to dinner with Ben, Linds, and the girls on Friday evening, and then heading back to Rochester Saturday morning.

Regarding my uneasiness: Frank and I get to bed around 9:00 the night before the first day of our hike. Our alarm is set for 4:30 so that we can be up and dressed in time to catch the 5:00 van ride to the trailhead. I wake up at 2:30 not feeling good. It's like a stomach flu. Then I feel chills and shortness of breath (maybe from the 8,000-foot altitude.) It's a mental challenge to stay calm, but I'm able to get back to sleep. On the van ride, we pick up a couple of lodge employees. One, a woman, asks Frank and me what our plans are for the day. We tell her it's our first time hiking across the Grand Canyon. She begins to say something about seeing trouble ahead for us (she must have possessed some psychic powers), when her coworker from the back seat pipes up with, "Now Wanda Jean, you stop right there." Given my state of mind, I was glad he had her put a halt to whatever she was about to say.

The hike to the bottom of the canyon went well. We saw only one rattlesnake, and the constant downhill pounding didn't cause any leg or foot pains. The last mile or two before reaching the canyon floor seemed to take us quite a while to complete. I was relieved to come around a bend and see the Bright Angel Campground, where we pitched our tent and enjoyed a delicious steak dinner. We visited with a woman sitting at a picnic table in the shade. She was a teacher from the Midwest. When I asked what book she was reading, she showed me the cover: *Grand Canyon Deaths*. My trepidation meter took another jump.

The Grand Canyon—truly a place that makes you feel small in the best of ways

It was a blazing hot one hundred and two degrees on the canyon floor. We woke at 4:00 AM, broke camp, ate our family-style breakfast at the Phantom Ranch Lodge, and were on the trail by 5:40. The 9.6-mile hike with 4,500 feet of climb went exceptionally well. I was pleased to finish fresh and strong. We celebrated our hike completion with a milkshake and a Coke and later in the afternoon enjoyed a fine dinner at the El Tovar dining room. The next morning, Frank and I drove to Sedona to meet our wives, and Jeanine and I flew back to Rochester. I will be forever grateful to Frank for making this hike happen.

Running
Still running after all these years

Running the Clear Lake (Iowa) Lake Race, a half marathon, with Greg Caucutt in the early 1980s

I don't remember when I first broke into a jog, but it must have been not too long after I learned to walk. In grade school gym class, I usually was the speediest in the running races. Steve Sorensen was pretty fast, too; he and I usually finished first and second in any of our competitions. I ran as a youngster mainly because I could get from point A to point B faster by running than I could by walking. Speed came naturally to me. It served me well in high school track, and it was the key ingredient in my doing well in the other sports I've written about in this book. I was quick, too. I not only had straight-ahead speed, but I could zig and zag with the best of them. A spring highlight for me each year would be getting a new pair of Keds tennis shoes. Those shoes made me feel faster and lighter on my feet than the year before. Even today, there's something about a new pair of running shoes that makes me remember what it felt like to be young.

My freshman and sophomore years in high school, I didn't try out for our track team. I made the team and lettered, though, my junior and senior years. We had spring track followed by summer baseball, so track provided something to do while I waited for my true love, baseball, to begin. Dad used to kid me because I'd drive our '51 Chevy from school to track practice about two miles away. He thought running to and from practice should have been part of my workout.

High school track team, my junior year. I am second from the left in the second row. Friends Roger Ashland and Steve Sorensen are in the middle of the back row and far right in the front row.

THE OLDER I GET THE BETTER I WAS

Dave Long was our track coach. (He went on to become Secretary of Education for the State of California.) Race distances were measured then in yards rather than meters. My best times were 5.8 seconds in the 50-yard dash, 11.3 seconds in the 100-yard dash, and 25 seconds in the 220-yard dash. The open 440 was too long for me; I wasn't big enough or strong enough to run that far all out. My best events were relays, the 440, 880, and distance medley. In my junior year, I ran on a team that set the school mile medley relay record of 3:48.3. We beat the previous record of 3:50.0 set in 1960 by Richard Ashland, John Davis, Jut Hughes, and Dave Bergmann. Bob Satter and I ran the 220-yard legs, Jim Leonard the 440-yard leg, and Roger Mayland the final 880 yards. The next year, I ran on a team that broke the record again with a time of 3:46.2. Steve Sorensen and I ran the 220 legs, Roger Wass the 440 leg, and Roger Mayland the 880. Mayland was the main reason we set the records; he was a hard-working, talented runner. In the 1960s, many long-distance runners were looked upon as "different." They ran many training miles. They were loners, some a bit off beat. Some summer days, I ran from my grandparents' farmhouse down the gravel road west to Highway 107. It was about a mile round trip, and it seemed a long way to me. I much preferred the sprint distances to longer runs. As the years went on, I ran longer and longer distances so that a mile didn't seem as long.

Our record-setting mile medley relay team: Roger Wass, Steve Sorensen, me, Roger Mayland

Our track meets started at the end of March with the State Indoor Meet and ran until the State Outdoor Meet at the end of May. In between we ran in the Eagle Relays (Eagle Grove), Valley Relays (Des Moines), Clear Lake Relays, Dickenson Relays (Cedar Falls), Bison Relays (Buffalo Center), Comet Relays (Charles City), Algona Relays,

Bronco Relays (Belmond), District Relays, and our Conference Relays. Track team members received points for finishing first, second, or third in individual and team events. Looking through my track ribbons, team stats, and newspaper clippings, I was surprised to see how many points I contributed to the team. During my junior year, only four of our twenty-two–member team scored one hundred points or more. I was the second highest point getter: The top four were Larry Shropshire (137), me (134), Jim Leonard (121), and Bob Satter (118).

We began track practices in the high school gym in early spring before the snow melted. We ran laps, ran sprints, and practiced our starts using starting blocks placed against the gym walls. I feel I was a good team member, practiced hard, and ran well in the meets. Though I didn't coast, I think I could have pushed myself to train harder, which would have produced even better results in the meets.

Our relay teams spent many hours practicing baton handoffs. Timing was everything. The waiting runner was in a marked zone in which the handoff from the incoming runner had to occur. The receiving runner had to start in advance so that he would be almost in full stride when he put his hand back and down to accept the baton from the incoming runner. Smooth handoffs were key to having faster times and gaining split-second advantages over the other teams. It was fun to watch the handoff from runner one to two, then two to three, and then three to four. When your anchor (typically the fastest guy on the team) got the baton, he turned on his all-out speed. Some anchors started ahead and stayed ahead. Some started behind and launched themselves past others to win. It was exciting to watch. I don't recall running anchor on any of my relay teams. Here are a few things I do recall:

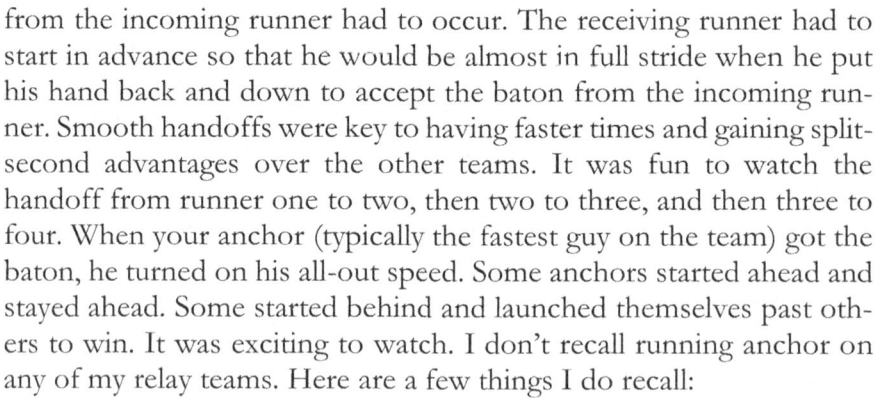

- The extremely lightweight leather track shoes (maybe Puma brand), which had extremely sharp spikes approximately one inch long. You didn't want to have anyone behind you slash their spikes into your calf. That thought (fear) was a huge motivator.

THE OLDER I GET THE BETTER I WAS

- Riding to track meets in two school vans. Dave Long drove one; I suppose our assistant track coach drove the other. Why do I remember that Alyn Holstad, a good hurdler and a goofy guy, would delight in showing us that he could squirt water (tears) out of his eyes?
- The Bison Relays in Buffalo Center (which we won) when it snowed and sleeted the entire meet. We were freezing cold in our skimpy little track uniforms.

In hindsight, I'm sorry I didn't run track all four years, but I'm thankful for the good memories I have of competing as a junior and senior.

During my college years and through the 1970s after I started with IBM, I ran for exercise but not competitively. I was busy with other sports: tennis, volleyball, racquetball, bicycling, softball, and more. On most IBM business trips, I would pack my running shoes and sweats for jogging before or after the workdays. Rarely would you see anyone going out for—or coming back from—a run. I would sneak in hotel back doors and ride in empty elevators to avoid drawing attention. When Jerry Will and I roomed together in Rochester and rented the Pump House (the house at the bottom of the hill behind the Plummer House), I would jog from there to Jeanine's apartment at Heritage Manor. She would have the air conditioning cranked up high. I would flop down for a while on a towel she had spread out on the living room floor, and then we'd hop in the pool.

My running intensity picked up in the 1970s when several friends got caught up in the marathon craze. Friends I'd run with included Greg Caucutt, Bob Waite, Rod Morlock, Keith Fisher, Dale Dahl, Ron Fess, and Mike Tomashek. They trained for and ran many marathons. We would run over the lunch hour during the week and on many weekend mornings (often meeting at Greg's house for a six- or eight-mile loop). Bob Waite and I ran the exercise stations circuit at the IBM park during noon breaks, too. IBM thoughtfully had a shower installed, but it wasn't air conditioned, so on hot, humid days, our white shirts would be soaked with sweat as we headed back to our offices.

10K Races

I probably ran more miles with Greg Caucutt than any of my other running friends. He and I really enjoyed running 10Ks (6.2 miles) together. When Greg and I got hooked on them, our goal always was to run each one in under forty minutes. One time, Dad and I went to the track at Soldiers Field where he timed me running a 10K. I finished under forty minutes, which I still feel today was quite an accomplishment. Following are some of my 10K races and times; I'm sure Greg ran in each of these, too.

May 8, 1982: Rochester IBM Club Spring Fun Run 10K: 39:49

May 25, 1983: The Rochester Life Run 10K: 38:13 (I finished twelfth out of seventy runners.)

October 12, 1983: IBM Watson Trophy 10K Run: 37:47 (I finished second in the Intermediate bracket and fifth overall.)

May 4, 1984: Rochester Life Run 10K: 38:00 (I finished thirty-fourth out of three hundred and forty-one runners.) A footnote: Bob Bardwell, whom I have gotten to know through helping him with his memoir, beat me by three seconds in this race and placed first in the race's wheelchair division. Bob is founder and director of Ironwood Springs Christian Ranch near Rochester.

The Frigid 8

For a few years, Greg and I ran in the Eau Claire, Wisconsin, annual Frigid 8 race, a hilly eight-miler held in December. In 1984 we finished in fifty-one minutes and fifty-five seconds, an average of 6½ minutes per mile. I had never run that far that fast.

Half Marathons and Marathons

Over the years, I completed several half marathons (13.1 miles). Clear Lake sponsored its inaugural half marathon run around the lake on June 6, 1981. They called it the Lake Race. I ran with Steve Sorensen, Bob Cline, and Mike Callanan. I don't have a record of my time. The next year, Greg Caucutt and I ran and finished in one hour and thirty-one minutes. In 1983, Greg and I ran again. I don't recall that time, probably slower than 1982 because I hit the wall blocks before the finish line, developed leg cramps, and hobbled my way to the finish line. I'm not sure how many more years the Lake Race continued, but with Tyler's birth in 1983, things got busy and I don't recall entering the race again. I'm sure glad, though, that I completed those three circles of my home-town lake.

I clocked my best half-marathon time—one hour twenty-seven minutes and sixteen seconds—at the Steamboat Days Race in Winona on June 30, 1983. Running conditions were ideal: a flat course, no wind and seventy degrees. Greg and I ran it together, stride for stride; it remains my personal best half-marathon time, and it gave me much respect for those who can run a marathon in three hours or less.

Greg and several other friends ran multiple marathons. They put in hours and hours of training that began months before a race. The race itself took much out of a person. One could expect to hit the wall at the twenty-mile mark no matter how good of shape you were in, and you just toughed it out from there. Given how grueling I found 10Ks and half marathons to be, my goal in life became to "never run a marathon." I am pleased to say that I've continued to meet that goal. Jeanine and I cheered Lindsey (our daughter-in-law) on to finish her Grandma's Marathon in Duluth (in 2014), and I "helped" Ron Fess run his marathon per the story that follows.

Ben cools me down after I finish the Lake Race half marathon in 1983.

Ron Fess and I ran together often. To mark his fortieth birthday, he entered the Twin Cities Marathon. It would be his first ever. He asked if I'd consider joining him at the twenty-mile mark, where many marathoners hit the wall, and run with him for three or four miles to offer encouragement, and then slip into the crowd a mile or so before the finish line. How could I say no?

Early that beautiful crisp fall morning, Jeanine and I began our drive from Rochester to Minneapolis; it was about the time that Ron started running the marathon. We were nearing the designated spot where I would join him when Jeanine shouted, "Look, there's Ron!" I saw his head bobbing along in a sea of runners. We pulled over, I hopped out and stripped off my sweats, and without a single stretch or warm-up began sprinting down the road to catch up with him. In short order I was by his side. He was glad to see me and was doing fine, setting a steady pace.

"Helping" Ron Fess (center of photo) complete his first marathon

Because of my lack of a warm-up and the rush to catch him, in a block or two I developed an excruciating side ache; it felt like I was running with a knife stuck in my stomach. It's been said that we all should have at least one person in our lives we don't want to disappoint. Well, at that point in my life, the one person I didn't want to disappoint was running right by my side at a much faster clip than I would have liked.

"Ron," I gasped. "I think I'm going to have to stop." Mind you, I had been running two blocks; he had been running twenty miles.

"Ransom," he said ... (he always called me—and most of his other friends—by their last names; I took it as a term of endearment). "Ransom, suck it up, and let's keep moving." Well, suck it up I did; the pain miraculously subsided so that I could run my four miles with him; and Ron completed his first of multiple marathons. For years, Ron and I joked about my "helping him" accomplish such a significant milestone in his running life.

Still Running After All These Years
Running is a form of meditation, a way to find yourself and get to know the real you better. I remember a runner describing the feeling that comes over a person while running. He said that for him it feels as if

his head has become detached from his body and is just gliding along, enjoying the ride. I know when I'm deep in thought while running, the time and miles just melt away, as if I no longer sense the passing of time but am just aware of being.

Of all of my sporting activities, running will be the one I will miss the most when I can no longer do it. Therefore, I approach each run with the goal to enjoy it rather than to just get it over with. I savor the feelings of putting one foot in front of the other and moving on down the road, the days when nothing (knees, hips, ankles) hurts. In 1980, then thirty-one years old, I timed myself running a mile just to see how fast I could finish one. I ran a 6-minute mile on May 14, a 5:44 on May 18, and a 5:29 on May 25. In October 2020, I wondered how fast I could run a mile; I hadn't timed myself in a long time. (I usually jog three miles at a leisurely pace and don't pay any attention to my time.) I clocked in at eight minutes and twenty-three seconds—not too bad for an old guy. Though I'm running slower each year, I want to enjoy every run that I'm healthy enough and able enough to do, because the day I outlive my ability to run will be a sad one. When I hang up my running shoes, I want to be sure I never took a mile I've jogged for granted.

I saved the following column that Donald Kaul wrote in the 1970s for the *Des Moines Register* newspaper:

I met a remarkable man the other day; I think he changed my life. It was on the bike path near my house, during my morning run. I'd just started when I passed this old man going in the opposite direction. I mean he was old—76, 103—somewhere in there. He walked with a cane, at a pace so slow as to be almost imperceptible. I smiled and said hello as I whooshed by, but he didn't seem to notice.

"Poor old fellow's in bad shape," I said to myself. "I hope I never get that way." I didn't give him another thought.

It's a funny thing. You'd think that when you run every day, you'd run pretty much the same every day. Not true. Some days you can run; some days you can't. This was one of the days I couldn't. My mind kept saying, "Glide! Glide!" but my legs kept saying, "Stomp, stomp." I just couldn't get the old machine up to speed.

I ran to the end of the bike path, turned around, and started back; the harder I tried the worse I seemed to run.

"I'm going to give this up," I remember thinking. "I get up and punish myself every morning and what do I get? I couldn't make the mile relay team of the DAR."

I trudged on—and I mean that literally—to the end of the path. I got there just as the old man whom I'd passed a half-hour earlier arrived. He'd been about 300 yards up the path when I first saw him. He got to the end of the path, reached into his pocket, pulled out a stopwatch, and hit the stop button. Then he looked at his time and nodded.

Nodded!

It was beautiful. If God hates quitters, He must love that old man. I know I do. I want to be like him when I grow up.

And I'm not quitting running. If a 10-minute mile is the best you can do, it's a damn good time.

I look at it the Kaul column much differently today than when I read it in the 1970s. I'm now much closer to being the "old guy" that he writes about. And like him, I'm not going to quit either.

Keep on Keeping On

*The only thing I knew how to do was to keep on keepin' on,
like a bird that flew; tangled up in blue.*
– Bob Dylan, Tangled up in Blue

My mother died at age seventy-one; Dad made it to ninety-three. Now seventy-two, I consider myself on the home stretch and not sure how long that stretch will be. The good news is that I'm still in the game. When I look back to my earlier years, I'm amazed at the energy I had and how many activities I could fit into a day. Here are a few journal entries to that point:

April 28, 1976: Super nice day. Gary (Allar) and I play tennis, then a softball game against Lobster House, a Camp Olson meeting at the YMCA, and a racquetball game at the Y with Jim Graddy. Eggs and pancakes at home at 10:30 PM. I added a note: Too busy a night.

June 27, 1976: Up at 6 AM. Took Willie (our springer spaniel) for a run. Dad and I played three sets of tennis. Then breakfast. Golfed with Sue; Dad and I played three more sets of tennis. Lunch. Went to golf driving range and then home to play more tennis with Jim Gilkinson.

Sept 29, 1976: Tennis with Greg Caucutt (5:00 to 6:15 PM). Racquetball with Tim Ryan (6:30 to 7:15 PM). Walked with Jeanine to Mr. Steak, had dinner, and walked back (a round trip of several miles) from 7:45 to 10:00 PM.

May 2, 1980: Ron Fess and I played tennis at 6 AM (IBM Park). I ran at noon from the YMCA, took a half day of vacation, and played more tennis at the outdoor club. Supper at the Gilkinsons.

July 6, 1980: Two sets of tennis at Slatterly Park, walked two and a half miles with Jeanine, ran six miles on the Douglas Trail, went to movie (Urban Cowboy), burgers on the grill for supper.

July 11, 1980: Hot and humid (one hundred plus degrees). Two sets of tennis at IBM courts. Ran IBM fitness course. Lunch with Jeanine at John Barleycorn. Washed car. Went to driving range. Racquetball at Supreme Court. Steaks on the grill.

July 23, 1988: Eighteen holes of golf with Dave Winkle and Jim Gilkinson. Three sets of tennis with Scott Littin (I won 6–0, 6–0,

6–3), then two sets of tennis with Suresh (he's very good, and I win 6–2, 6–4).

No longer have I that much energy, but I haven't yet given in to the afternoon nap urge. I plan to keep moving, doing what my health allows, until the day I die. One thing I've done throughout my life is associate with positive, energetic, young-thinking people, of all ages—in and out of sports. As a memoirist, I work often with humble, accomplished people ten, twenty, and more years older than me, and my associations with them have reminded me that relative to them, I'm still young. More often than not, I am inspired from my working with them. A month ago, I began helping a client, age ninety-eight, and his wife write their life stories. He had lived and died baseball and dreamt of making the major leagues. World War II came along, however, and dashed those dreams. When he returned home in 1945, he was needed in the family banking business. He tried out for a minor league team in St. Cloud but didn't make the cut. Instead, he played ball on town teams. At age *seventy-two*, he was on a team in a thirty-five-and-over league. At age *ninety*, he was still suited up and playing some town ball. Why should I feel old at seventy-two?

Some days I wonder if I have devoted too much time to sporting activities. I could have invested more of those hours feeding the poor, striving for world peace, or combating climate change. Those thoughts pass quickly, though, when I realize what I've gained from my athletic endeavors; I'm in good shape and a better person because of them.

I need exercise the way a fish needs water. Also, I'm an observer, and I noticed that people would often gain weight and fall out of shape at several checkpoints in life: going to college, starting their first job, getting married, and having children. I committed myself to staying fit at each milestone. In college, at the end of a long day of classes, dead tired, I would head to the Beyer Hall gymnasium for a workout—paddleball, basketball, tennis, whatever. Many days I didn't feel I had the energy to do it, but I'd forge ahead anyway. After a workout, I felt a world of difference, energized, ready for supper and then a few hours of hitting the books. I was fortunate to marry Jeanine, a sports enthusiast and a physically fit person herself. We both loved hiking, biking, walking, tennis, skiing, and more, so I had a partner who valued being fit as much as I did. When Ben and Tyler came along in the 1980s, my commitment to fitness remained as strong as ever. I still love the feeling of being trim. I weigh about one hundred and forty pounds, which is five pounds more than my high school and college weight. My waist measures thirty inches, about an inch more than in 1972 when Jeanine and I were married. My resting heart rate, at my fittest, was in the mid-forties beats per minute. I remember health checkups where the nurse taking my pulse would look at me and say, "You're a runner, aren't you?"

Exercise has been cheap therapy. Working for IBM was stressful at times, particularly during my years in management. Sports provided escapes from whatever might have been worrying me and kept me on a calm, even keel. In the middle of a squash rally that leaves me gasping for breath, I can't worry about much that lies beyond the next point. When I jog, my mind clears and I come up with possible solutions to problems, and I work through things that are making me anxious or angry. Running helps me cope with sadness, too. I remember jogs after our son Tyler died in 1985 and in the summer of 1997 after Mom died and Dad was hospitalized with depression where I would cry while I ran, the only time I allowed myself tears. This year of the pandemic, 2020, has been a difficult one to get through. Walking and jogging daily are helping me cope.

Through sports, I've learned how to be a good team player. My personality is such that I like to help others do their best. That's why volleyball suited me so well. I was the little guy popping the nice sets that the big guys could hammer to the floor. Or batting leadoff, getting on base to steal a bag or two and have the power hitters bring me home. There's a hard-to-put-into-words feeling of playing on a team that's clicking on all cylinders. Turning the smooth double play, the opponents volleyball serve that we bump, set, and spike perfectly for a point, a long doubles racquetball rally where you, your partner, and the other team are moving cooperatively yet competitively, as if in a choreographed ballet. It's easy to get along with your teammates when things are going smoothly. Not so when they are not. When I coached youth baseball, I would remind my players that we had an opponent on the ropes when their team members started fighting amongst themselves. "Never show the other team that we're upset with one another," I'd say. And we wouldn't.

With Ben (and trophies) in the mid-1980s

I believe you learn more about a person's character from their losses than from their wins. The YMCA sportsman of the year trophy I received in 1976 means much to me. I have tried my best, win or lose, to always play hard and fair and never let any game's frustration get the better of me. My closest friendships I've made through sports are with people who share those values. On his deathbed, Ty Cobb, the Hall-of-Fame baseball player, said if he had it all to do over again, he would have had more friends. If I have time for deathbed comments, thankfully, that one won't be necessary. The trophies and awards have been nice, but what I treasure most are the memories and friendships I have made through sports.

About the Author

Mike Ransom is a professional writer who specializes in memoir, biography, and company history. He lives in Rochester, Minnesota, with his wife, Jeanine. Since 1997, he has written more than twenty memoirs in addition to the Rochester Golf and Country Club history (*Celebrating a Century*), the Rochester Charter House Retirement Community history (*Our Roots and Our Spirit*), and numerous articles for magazines and newsletters. Mike enjoys reading, music, movies, coffee shops, jogging, St. Paul, Grand Marais, and time spent with Jeanine, their son (Ben), his wife (Lindsey), and their daughters (Greta, Ellie, and Hattie). More about Mike and his writing can be found at www.mransomwriter.com.

Made in the USA
Coppell, TX
06 June 2022